Lambeth architecture 1914-1939

Edmund Bird & Fiona Price

**London Borough of Lambeth and the
Lambeth Local History Forum**

Published in 2012 by Lambeth Archives and Lambeth Local History Forum
Lambeth Archives, 52 Knatchbull Road, London SE5 9QY
www.lambeth.gov.uk/Services/LeisureCulture/LocalHistory/Archives.
www.landmark.lambeth.gov.uk/
Printed by Pitney Bowes
© London Borough of Lambeth and the authors 2012. All images are copyright London Borough of Lambeth and the authors unless otherwise stated. ISBN 978-0-9543173-9-3

Acknowledgements

The authors are grateful to the following people and organisations for permitting the use of their images:

Doug Black, Head of Lambeth's Conservation & Urban Design Team, for images of the Prince of Wales fleurs-de-lis and ABC Streatham medallions (p6), the art deco house (p 73) and the stained glass window in Streatham baths (p92); Don Clarke of the Old Grammarians (the former Battersea Grammar School, Streatham) for use of top image: www.oldgrammarians.co.uk (p35).

London Transport Museum (www.ltmuseum.co.uk); for Clapham Common Underground Station (p54) and Brixton Hill Tram Depot (p55); Eva Tyler and Jamie Gili of Pullman Court Residents Group for image of Pullman Court (p69 bottom); MRJ Rundell & Associates (Architects) for the photos on p75 (www.rundellassociates.com); Rev Ian Gilmour of Holy Redeemer Church in Streatham for use of two images (p76); Daily Herald Archive/ National Media Museum/ SSPL for photo of Quin & Axten (p81); National Railway Museum for photo of WH Smith's bookstall at Waterloo (p95); Beacon Bingo HQ, Milton Keynes for the photo of Streatham Hill Theatre Foyer picture (p47); The Cinema Theatre Association (www.cinema-theatre.org.uk); for images of Streatham Regal Cinema (p41), Streatham Gaumont Cinema (p45), Waterloo News Theatre (p95) and two images of Camberwell Odeon Cinema (p94) and John Bradshaw/ www.transport-of-delight.com for the photo of the Waterloo Signal Box (p89).

We are grateful for the assistance of Margaret & Kenneth Bird, Doug Black (Head of Conservation & Urban Design, London Borough of Lambeth), Elain Harwood (English Heritage), Charles O'Brien, Clive Polden (CTA Archivist), Len Reilly, John Newman and Phillip Norman, (Lambeth Archives) for their invaluable contributions in sourcing material and proof reading. Also to Tom Brown, Street Naming & Numbering/Data Support, Lambeth Council for composition of the location map, Steve Lake at Whatever Design and Pitney Bowes printers.

Contents

Foreword by Bridget Cherry 5

Introduction 7

Lambeth Town Hall – assembly hall and extension 14

Other public buildings 19

Education 31

Public health 36

Leisure and entertainment 40

On the move 54

Housing 57

Ecclesiastical buildings 76

Commercial 79

Lost inter-war buildings of Lambeth 86

Index of buildings 96

Foreword by Bridget Cherry

Architectural historian, author and editor of Pevsner's Buildings of England 2: London: South

Lambeth has a long history but its appearance today owes much to the building activity which took place between the wars. If one travels south from the site of the old Lambeth village on the banks of the Thames, through Clapham or Brixton to the heights of Norwood or the leafy suburbs of Streatham, it is clear that that the identity of local centres is still reinforced by the confident department stores, exuberant cinemas and cheerful pubs built in the 1920-30s. The civic pride marked by the creation of the borough at the start of the century led on to provision of better services and living conditions. One can still find public services housed in handsome buildings that added dignity to their surroundings; this was also a period of progressively designed schools and a lido. A vast quantity of new housing replaced the slums of the inner suburbs, while distinctive private blocks of flats sprang up in the spacious suburban areas further south.

This was a period which revelled in diversity of styles. The showmanship of the Edwardian era gave way to a more restrained form of classically inspired architecture, favouring plain walls with carefully proportioned windows, as in the carefully massed extensions to Lambeth Town Hall. A friendly domestic Georgian was the inspiration for buildings such as the South London Hospital for Women, and the attractive housing built by the Duchy of Cornwall estate and in many of the sturdy blocks of flats put up by the LCC. Progressive design, influenced by continental modernism, looked afresh at window arrangements, as in the light and airy Jessop Primary School Herne Hill, or explored more abstract patterning; insistent brick banding and fine sculpture dominates the massive Fire Brigade headquarters on the Albert Embankment, while the former Granada Cinema in Wandsworth Road makes play with strong horizontals and verticals. Other cinemas adopted a lively assortment of styles, from the flamboyant baroque of the Brixton (still with its interior complete) to the elegantly streamlined curves of the Streatham Regal. Perhaps the least well known building type of this period is the private apartment block, distinguished from council housing by exteriors featuring emphatic balconies and a variety of materials.

A special delight in exploring the buildings of this period is the unexpected detail; the fine sculpture on the Town Hall extension, the colourful Egyptian detail of the tiny Reliance Arcade at Brixton Market; the surprising jazzy brickwork around the angular doors at Henry Fawcett Primary school, Kennington, or the grand foyer of the Streatham Hill Theatre.

This book demonstrates the wealth and wide range of interesting buildings from this period and catalogues many wonderful buildings such as the WH Smiths and Doulton buildings on the Albert Embankment that were destroyed 30 years ago but which may well have been listed and cherished had they survived. Some of those illustrated here, such as the Brockwell Park Lido, have been excellently restored, but others have a more uncertain future and deserve to be cherished.

Location Map

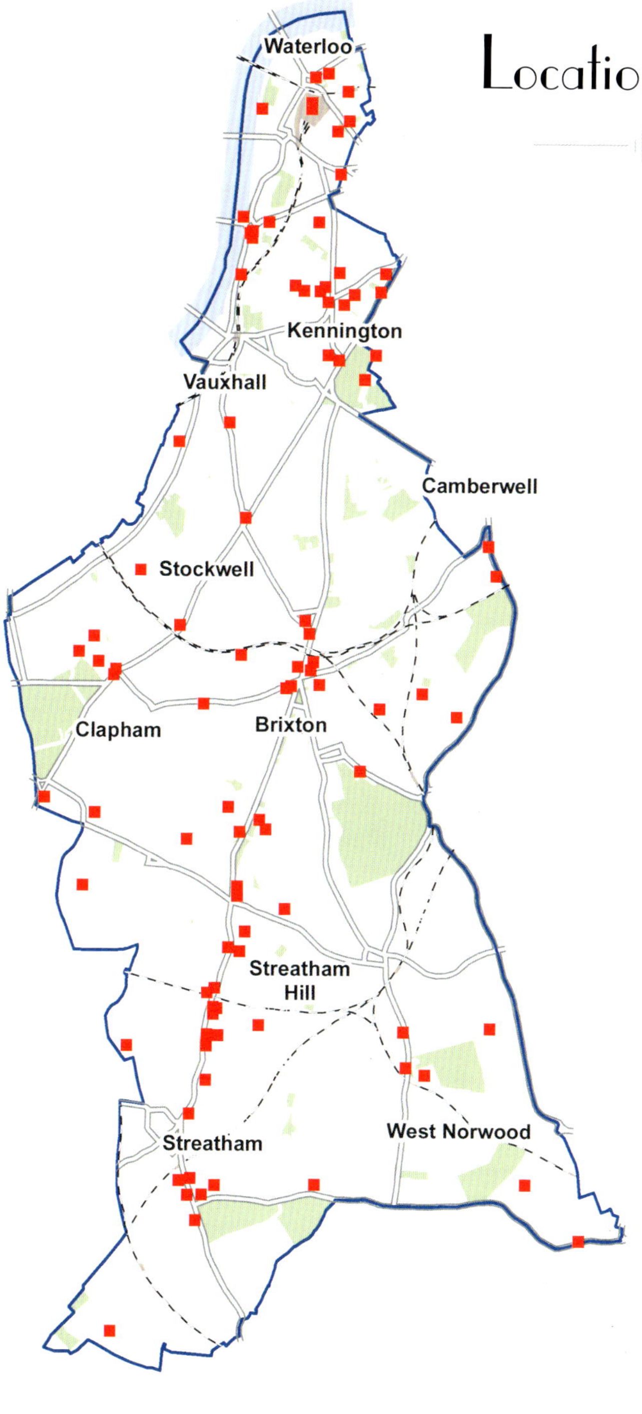

Fleur-de-lis on the Prince of Wales pub in Brixton and medallions from the ABC Cinema Streatham

Introduction

This book takes the story forward from our previous "Edwardian Splendours of Lambeth" which covered the period 1901-1914 and which was published in 2010; here we will be appraising the architectural legacy of the 1920s and 1930s, between the First and Second World Wars. The Borough of Lambeth had been formed in 1900 and in the inter-war years comprised a smaller area than today.

The historic Lambeth neighbourhoods of Waterloo, Kennington, Vauxhall, Stockwell, West Camberwell, Brixton, Herne Hill and West Norwood, were joined by Streatham and Clapham after the local government reorganisation of 1965, transferred from Wandsworth. For the purposes of this series of books, the architecture of the present-day borough is assessed, including Clapham and Streatham.

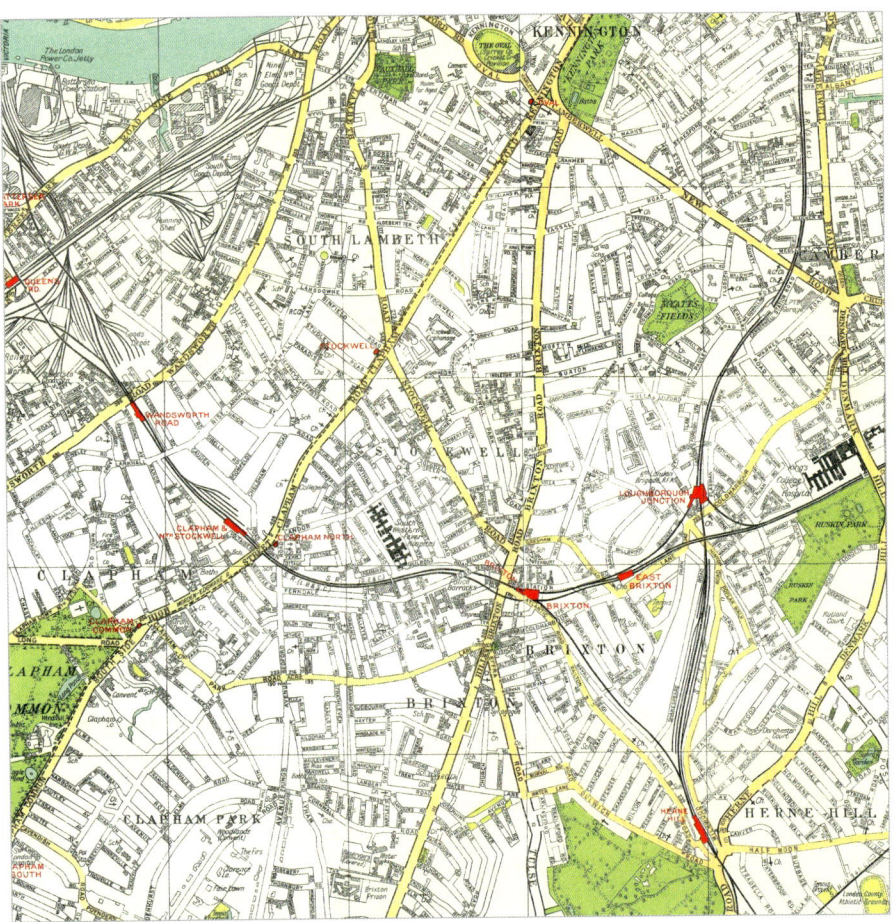

We look first at the 1930s extensions to Lambeth Town Hall which remains the key symbol of the borough's civic pride. Then we move on to appraise other landmarks of the 1920s and 1930s in the borough that all reflect the gradual improvements in the standard of living, new leisure and shopping trends, new transport links and further residential growth. These structures give a fascinating insight into the political, social and economic character of the inter-war years, which produced buildings dedicated to the improvement in health, housing, education, transport and leisure opportunities for the citizens of Lambeth during this period.

This map shows Brixton, West Camberwell, Clapham, Herne Hill, Stockwell and the Oval in 1936. Note the former East Brixton Station, closed in 1976.

The First World War caused a hiatus in construction which ensured that Edwardian and inter-war styles were markedly different from each other. London only really began to develop again in the 1920s when the world was a very different place. The architecture changed from the elaborate classical styles of the Edwardian era to plainer and more restrained styles such as the simple 20th century Georgian idiom, the colourful art deco influence and early examples of the Modern Movement.

New construction technologies made taller buildings possible during the 20th century. Building by means of a steel frame skeleton became a widely-used construction method in the first quarter of the century. It not only enabled buildings to get taller, but also to increase in bulk. Thanks to steel framing, the streets of central London took on a new, large scale in the years between the wars. Shops became department stores, office blocks became large corporate headquarters and cinemas became glamorous picture palaces.

By 1926 the national economy was in serious trouble and the ten-day General Strike of May 1926 affected the majority of the population in some way. London largely escaped the depression that decimated industries elsewhere in Britain during the 1930s. However another threat dominated this period - the threat of fascism in Europe.

War with Germany began to look inevitable and the decade ended with preparation to evacuate London's children to the comparative safety of the countryside.

Nonetheless by the time of the coronation of King George VI and Queen Elizabeth in 1937 the citizens of Lambeth were beginning to enjoy a markedly better standard of living as the efforts of the government, the London County Council and the Borough of Lambeth to actively tackle poverty and poor public health and improve education and employment opportunities bore fruit. This image shows Lambeth Town Hall decorated for the coronation in May 1937.

Housing in inter-war Lambeth

Between 1911 and 1931 Lambeth's population was still growing. From 408,000 in 1911 it peaked at 421,000 in 1931 though by 1951 it had fallen to 347,000. The enfranchisement of men over 21 and of women over 30 in 1918 (and women over 21 in 1928) forced housing up the political agenda. One of the few issues on which governments sought the opinion of women was housing. Homes were needed but prices had risen greatly during the war, ensuring that these would not be built by private investors. In 1919, amid growing social unrest caused by poor housing and unemployment, riots against the police, and strikes by police and soldiers, the government decided to put significant national funds into house building. In the 1920s the LCC initially concentrated on building cottage estates in the suburbs, but with the advent of a Labour Government in 1929 it began to look for land for housing in inner London where people needed to live nearer to their workplaces. Despite the efforts of the LCC, pockets of abject poverty in London persisted and in 1929 the Poor Law system with its workhouses and boards of guardians were abolished and the responsibility for welfare and healthcare were transferred to local authorities. Efforts were made by local councils to keep families together and the wealthier boroughs were at last forced to contribute to the support of people in the poorer boroughs by means of the rating system. By 1938 council-owned housing stock reached 11%. However, the "new" idea of home ownership created the real revolution in inter-war housing.

By 1938 35% of all homes were owner-occupied compared with barely 10% before 1914. This image shows **Crown Lane Gardens** (near Streatham Common) under construction in c1935. Two-storey flats are grouped around attractive communal gardens and are still popular today. They have flat roofs, tile hung walls and art deco doorways.

Times had changed since the Great War and fewer women went into service or were expected to have servants to do the work in big houses, but social mores still largely prevented married women from working outside the home.

Widespread electricity in London heralded the advent of electric gadgets to aid work in the home and new homes were often sold complete with washing machines, vacuum cleaners and cookers. In 1923 councils were allowed to offer mortgages to prospective purchasers or at least to guarantee loans which boosted the private housing market. Building Societies flourished as the economy slumped and they became the safest places to keep savings. House prices hit an all-time low in the 1930s and houses were sold in almost the same way as other mass-produced

goods. The inter-war years saw the emergence of major speculative building firms such as Richard Costain, John Laing, Taylor Woodrow and George Wimpey.

Critics derided the spread of their "Tudorbethan" estates and accused developers of "jerry-building". The quality of house-construction saw a marked increase in the 1930s with the introduction of 11-inch brickwork and cavity walls. However, the haphazard growth associated with the suburban dream created a problem of wasted land, the destruction of valuable open spaces and traffic chaos. The post-WWII development would see much more control by local and central government under the Ribbon Development Act of 1935 and the Town and Country Act of 1947. The declaration of war in 1939 was to slow the private housing boom which stopped completely in 1940.

Entertainment

There was a new mood in the post-war London of the 1920s. After the privations of war, many people were keen to seize any opportunity for leisure and self-indulgence. British life began to change rapidly, especially in terms of the commercialisation of entertainment and fashion (see photo below right of ladies apparel on display in Morley's Department Store in Brixton in c1925). The capital began to feel less traditional and more modern. War time restrictions were lifted and new sorts of entertainment were created – entrepreneurs opened clubs, restaurants and dance halls to cater for the new crazes: jazz and dancing.

Huge new picture palaces were built during the 1920s and 1930s, sending many of the old theatres and music halls into decline. The interiors were lavish affairs where anyone could be transported to a fantasy world all for the modest sum of 6d. The Great War had allowed women hitherto unknown freedoms and in return for hard-work, finally gained them the vote, cementing women's place in a "grown-up" society. However, the advent of cinema changed perceptions of women as domestic goddess, to those of sex siren *and* domestic goddess - a perception which was to be strengthened and used in the years of the great depression of the 1920s and 30s, as Britain struggled to reclaim jobs for the men and push women back to where they "belonged" in the home.

With keen interest in fresh air and sunshine, the 1930s was the golden age of lidos. Lambeth had two: one in Kennington Park which opened in 1931 (sadly demolished) and another in Brockwell Park (1937) which is still popular today. 'Wireless' radio was the technological marvel of the decade and it soon became accessible to the mass market. 1922 saw the first radio broadcast of the British Broadcasting Company (later the British Broadcasting Corporation) from premises in the Strand. This was broadcast to 36,000 license holders; by 1931 there were 4.3 million license holders and by 1939, nine million. Between 1936 and 1939 (when it was suspended due to war), black & white television was being broadcast for four hours per day. This helped to cement the importance of the place of the home in the British psyche.

Transport and communications

London in the 1930s became cleaner, more modern and efficient. It was increasingly a city of electric lighting and motor vehicles rather than gas lighting and horse-drawn transport. Horse drawn trams were completely phased out by 1915 and replaced by motor buses and electric trams. In 1926 the first double-decker bus with a covered top deck was introduced in London and this rapidly became the standard.

Trolley buses arrived in London in 1931 and began to replace the old trams with a smoother and quieter ride. Motor cars took off in a big way after the First World War with greater production bringing small cars within reach of many by 1935. Unfortunately driving was regarded as a sport, leading to over 7,000 fatalities in 1930 compared with 3,221 in 2004. In 1934 the Transport Minister, Leslie Hore-Belisha, promoting safety in motoring, introduced the pedestrian crossing with Belisha Beacons to London streets. This image shows a woman beside a bus by The Greyhound pub opposite Streatham Common in c1932.

The London Passenger Transport Board took over control of the underground railways and buses in 1933 as a way of bringing all the capital's transport providers together. The City and South London Railway Company had extended the Northern Line to Clapham in 1900 and in 1922 a major facelift began. This was completed in 1924 and a further extension to Morden completed in 1926.

In 1923 the myriad of different railway companies in Britain were merged into the Big Four, but Herbert Morrison (who was born in Lambeth) as Leader of the LCC and later transport minister in Ramsay Macdonald's Government, wanted to go further and nationalise the railways, which eventually occurred in 1948. The Southern Railway which from 1923 operated the suburban and mainline railways through Lambeth had rapidly electrified all its London commuter services by 1929. The re-building of Waterloo Station was completed in 1921, complete with a grand curving concourse, a tea room and buffet.

Telephones were also becoming very popular, leading to the complete automation of London's telephone exchanges by the General Post Office. It was in 1920 that telephone boxes were introduced to London's streets, the iconic K2 red phone box being designed by Sir Giles Gilbert Scott in 1926.

Economy and employment

After 1918, Britain's manufacturing economy saw a serious decline. The collapse of Britain's export market in textiles and an over-supply of goods for a short post-war consumer boom caused mass unemployment, class divisions, and protests such as the General Strike, the Hunger Marches and, especially in London, clashes with the British Fascists. London's docks, however resumed their role as the engine of London's wealth. The volume of imports and exports rose with the opening of the King George V Docks in 1921. In central London new office jobs were created by a new generation of British corporations and banks. There was, however, another side to the 1930s - the majority of people actually kept their jobs and because prices fell faster than wages the real value of incomes rose significantly between 1924 and 1935. One of the main results of this prosperity was the rise in house ownership. Consumerism developed and both middle- and working-class families sought to spend more of their income on minor luxuries.

This image of c1935 is of the Telephone Manufacturing Company's Hollingsworth Works in Martell Road in West Norwood, which were opened in 1915 to produce telephones, switchboards, electric clocks etc. This imposing building survives today (sadly without its clock) as the Parkhall Road Trading Estate.

Younger women, often employed in preference to older men due to their willingness to work for lower wages, could now emulate film stars thanks to the advent of cheap rayon and artificial silk; fashion became important and the use of cosmetics, especially lipstick rouge and eye shadow, became popular. Class barriers, whilst still remaining intact, generated less conflict than before due greater wealth resulting from economic growth and better education.

In 1923 Lambeth was 10th out of the 28 boroughs in terms of its number of factories. Medium and light engineering industries such as manufacture of printing machinery, lifts, car parts, household goods, building equipment, pressed metalwork and electrical equipment were all represented in the borough. Food industries, such as Waterloo Flour Mills, flourished in Lambeth, due to the proximity of the river for transport, as did light chemical industries producing surgical goods, patent medicines, drugs, and such like. Printers William Clowes & Sons Ltd. remained on the riverside until their premises were burnt out in the Blitz. Bowaters and the Eldorado ice cream works (whose site is now occupied by Bernie Spain Gardens) also remained through the 1930s; and lead shot continued to be made in the shot tower on the South Bank until 1949. Huge concrete warehouses were built in Waterloo such as those owned by Boots and WH Smiths. Along with the proliferation of white-collar jobs in the City, County Hall, completed in 1922 and hugely extended in the 1930s, provided much employment for residents of Lambeth.

Public Buildings, schools, churches and hospitals

Construction of public buildings such as County Hall resumed after a break during the First World War. There were new trends in the design of school and hospital buildings resulting in a proliferation of new or extended hospitals such as the South London Hospital for Women and the **Annie McCall Maternity Hospital** in Jefferies Road, (now the Stockwell Studios, pictured right which was listed Grade II in 2011). Inter-war Britain was fast becoming a healthier society; average life expectancy for men rose from 52 to 61 years between 1910 and 1938. Similarly, deaths of babies of less than 12 months fell from 110 to 55 per 1,000 between 1910 and 1938.

In 1918 the Maternity and Child Welfare Act required local authorities to establish infant welfare and natal clinics. Cod liver oil, iron and vitamin products were sold cheaply to mothers. Lambeth was one of the first of the London boroughs to open a Municipal Milk Depot. There were no antibiotics until 1941 but doctors became more confident in carrying out operations and other treatments.

Society after the First World War came to recognise childhood as an distinct period of life rather than viewing children as small grown-ups. The school leaving age was raised to 14 in 1918 but schooling for most children was still carried out in elementary schools, apart from those able to attend a grammar school. In 1926 the Hadow Report recommended that the school leaving age be raised to 15 and children change schools at 11 to continue their secondary education. This achieved some success as by 1938 two-thirds of children had some form of secondary education causing a flurry of school building particularly in the later 1930s. This photo shows **Jessop Primary** in 1938.

Few new churches were built in inner London in this period due to the great legacy of Victorian church-building, but many churches were built to serve the growing suburbs, e.g. the Holy Redeemer in Streatham Vale.

Public Buildings: Lambeth Town Hall Assembly Hall - Acre Lane - Grade II

The town hall was opened in 1908 by the Prince and Princess of Wales, who two years later became King George V and Queen Mary. Its architect, H. Austen Hall (by now in the partnership Whinney, Son and H. Austen Hall), was invited back nearly 30 years later to design extensions to the original building; the job architect was E.R. Silver. These comprised an extra storey to the Edwardian town hall, an assembly hall and an extension to the rear. Queen Mary, by this time the Queen Mother after the death of her husband King George V in 1936, was invited to return to Brixton to open these extensions on 14th October 1938 (see photos below).

The 1938 wing is an excellent example of how to extend an historic building. It uses the same palette of materials as the original Edwardian building of 1908 - red brick and stone dressings with a stone plinth and quoins - yet employs a simplified style. This represents a subtle updating resulting in a design very much of its time whilst respecting and complementing the original scale, massing and character of its host building.

The assembly hall is linked to the 1908 building by a symmetrical five-bay, three-storey facade, which has three set-back tripartite casements within round arches to the ground floor set between projecting single-range wings with stone plinths and quoins. Within the left hand projecting bay is a door with a large fanlight and moulded keystone. The second-floor band, bolection-moulded cornice and parapet are all highly effective in anchoring the extension to the older building in an almost seamless transition. The assembly hall has a five-bay range fronting Acre Lane with a stone balustrade above five metal-framed casement windows to the long committee room on the first floor. This frontage returns along Buckner Road with a smooth plinth of Portland stone with an elegant rounded corner. An art deco, cinema-style, metal canopy with recessed neon lighting extends over the three sets of double, wooden framed, glazed doors, which form the public entrance to the hall. The composition culminates in a fine corner tower which forms a landmark on Acre Lane, counter-balancing and complimenting the clock tower of the 1908 town hall. It is topped by a stone pediment above aediculed openings, and has a very practical use, ventilating the assembly hall below.

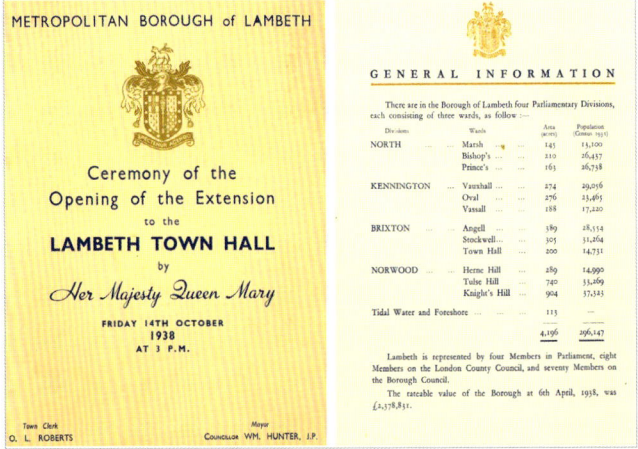

The interior

The outer lobby to the assembly hall (pictured below) is entered from the street via three pairs of glazed doors. It is lined with marble and has a coffered ceiling, original bronze uplighters and a timber and glass cinema-style paybox between the pairs of glazed doors leading into the inner vestibule. A commemorative stone inscribed in the marble side wall records the opening of the extension to the town hall by Queen Mary in 1938.

The elevation to Buckner Road is embellished with a handsome stone relief of a figure of 'youth' by the sculptor Denis Dunlop. Dunlop was a noted sculptor of the 1930s and 40s who also collaborated with architect Austen Hall on two other commissions, designing the bas-reliefs at the London Midland & Scottish Railway training college in Derby (also of 1938) and the figure of Mercury on the Bristol Aeroplane Company Headquarters (1936). Both are also listed Grade II.

The long inner lobby (left) retains its splendid circular glass pendant light fittings suspended from shallow concave domed insets - a pair of doors at the eastern end lead to the town hall corridor and those at the western end to an elegant art deco staircase with metalwork balustrade (pictured below and on the following page). This leads up to a first-floor committee room (now an office) with beautiful marble fireplaces at each end - one is pictured below left.

The assembly hall has highly original articulated timber panelling resembling a classical elevation of ashlar masonry (see image to right). This was a device of Scandinavian origins used in 1929 by architect Charles Holden at his London Transport Head Office at 55 Broadway for the most important floor occupied by the Chairman. This panelling incorporates elaborate metal grills to the heating system. The stage has a square-headed proscenium in the pared-down 1930s manner with a clock to one side. The timber-boarded floor is sprung for dancing and the inset ceiling has a patterned art deco style ventilation grille above the stage.

Other public buildings

County Hall - North and South Blocks - Belvedere Road - Locally Listed

The London County Council (LCC) was created in 1888, and the first phase of its grand riverside main building was built between 1912 and 1922. It is an Edwardian design but was largely completed after the First World War after the hostilities delayed construction. The riverside building was not finished until 1933 when the north wing was completed, housing a total of 3,700 staff. However even this did not provide sufficient accommodation for the rapidly expanding departments within the council so the LCC started planning two massive new extension blocks between the riverside building and York Road, known as the North and South Blocks. One of the most famous architects of the day, Sir Giles Gilbert Scott, was commissioned as consulting architect to work with the LCC's own architects department, headed by E.P. Wheeler and his successor F.R. Hiorns. These blocks were built between 1936 and 1939, linked by a grand single-storey stone gateway which incorporated stone from the recently demolished Waterloo Bridge (see photo below taken soon after their completion in 1939). The two blocks added offices for a further 1,550 staff, County Hall now accommodating 5,250 staff. They were further extended after the Second World War - a new wing on the far right of the photo below, fronting Westminster Bridge Road was completed over twenty years later in 1963 and the left hand block was extended along Chicheley Street in 1955-58, both enclosing the great courtyard seen below.

The top and bottom views to the left are looking up York Road with the South Wing in the foreground and the North Wing beyond. The top left image was taken in 1939, very soon after the completion of the main portion of the two blocks (before their extensions in the 1950s and 60s).

Note the kerb stones painted black and white in preparation for the Second World War, which improved road safety during the black-out. Both blocks are locally listed and lie within the South Bank Conservation Area.

The eight-storey elevations of Portland stone are very dignified and designed in the restrained George VI classical manner. The top floor is accommodated within giant tiled mansard roofs and lit by copper-clad dormer windows. All of the windows are metal Crittall casement windows. The elevations are carefully composed, with a very horizontal emphasis to the ground-floor plinth and cornice above the fifth floor, balanced by the very vertical emphasis of the first to fifth floors created by the regular rhythm of the windows. The outer corners of the blocks are canted with grand bronze entrance doors below arched windows with massive keystones. The entrances have magnificent octagonal lanterns mounted on tall circular section stone pillars with capitals standing like sentries either side of the doorways.

These two blocks narrowly escaped demolition proposals in the 1990s. However the low gateway structure that linked the North and South blocks was removed in c2000 to enable the creation of the new Forum Magna Square (see photo below) and the insertion of two new blocks of flats over restaurants, built over the courtyard. The North and South blocks were converted to flats.

Lambeth Fire Station and Brigade Headquarters - Albert Embankment - Grade II

This moderne style building on the Albert Embankment was until 2008 the London Fire Brigade Headquarters. It was built in 1937 by the LCC to the design of E.P. Wheeler, their chief architect, assisted by G. Weald. A giant stone crest of the LCC by sculptor F.P. Morton sits at the top of the central bay. The lavish sculpture with background of gold mosaic is by Gilbert Bayes. This is undoubtedly one of Lambeth's finest 1930s landmark buildings. It is a long rectangular block of eight storeys with a strong horizontal emphasis. Its steel frame is clad in brown-grey bricks in an English bond. The facade has facings of Portland stone to the ground and first floors, the full-width balcony to the first floor, the cornice to the top floor and on the central tower. The fire station has seven appliance bays with staff facilities such as mess rooms on the first and second floors. The upper floors were built as administrative offices and living accommodation for the firemen, but later were all used as offices. The rear elevation is even more dramatic comprising balconies on every floor facing the drill yard.

23 | Other public buildings

The tall drill tower (top left photo) and one of the original pair of observation prow balconies survive, (photo left) the other was lost in the 1980s as was the splendid bandstand (far left photo), to make way for the uninspiring control room. The view above taken in 1938 is little changed today except for the redevelopment of the neighbouring sites including the WH Smith building of 1933 to its left.

The main entrance hall is clad in marble with a geometric frieze. There are beautiful patterned grilles in the art deco style set within openings, and moving memorials dedicated to fire officers who lost their lives in the course of their duties in peace and war time. The marble relief depicting a fire-fighting scene is pictured above. The elegant staircases have bronze balustrades.

Interiors on the first and second floors include a mess room with beamed coffered ceiling and a panelled conference room with a fluted frieze. A full-height modern movement stair (pictured top right) connects the upper floors.

On the other side of Lambeth High Street is a now vacant lower block which used to accommodate a training school and workshops.

It is now proposed to convert the upper floors into private flats and redevelop the rear workshop block.

Gipsy Hill Police Station - Central Hill - Norwood

This police station dates from c1930 - it is a fusion of the two popular styles of this period. The red brick, stone dressings and slated roof are in the George V style, echoing elements of the 18th century Georgian influence. However the stone doorcase with the relief of the royal arms emblazoned above the individual lettering is very art deco, as is the stone tablet incorporating a glass display case for police posters on the street frontage.

This police station replaced the earlier mid-Victorian one which still survives, now in residential use and named Gipsy Hill House (No.12 Gipsy Hill).

Gipsy Hill police station is proposed for local listing.

Lambeth County Court - Cleaver Street - Kennington

Lambeth County Court is an elegant building opened in 1928. It is on a quiet side street between Cleaver Square and Kennington Road. It is of red brick embellished with superb stonework tablets between ground and first-floor windows and surrounding the central entrance, above which is the royal coat of arms.

The courthouse is typical of the inter-war period and is much more restrained than its predecessors of the Edwardian era but conveying a reserved dignity. Its symmetrical design, regular rhythm of window openings and well-detailed door-case all contribute to its imposing presence, respecting the scale and character of its largely early 19th century context and yet declaring its civic purpose.

The elaborate metal-framed casement windows incorporate the St Andrew's Cross, again a popular design of the period. The photo below dates from 1972. It is locally listed and lies within the Kennington Conservation Area.

War Memorial - Streatham Common Northside

In the years following the First World War, memorials to the fallen were erected in towns, villages and suburbs across Britain. Streatham was no exception and a fine memorial was unveiled on 14 October 1922 by General Sir Charles Munro, four years after the Armistice marked the end of the war.

The ceremony was attended by some 5,000 local residents. The memorial is of a bronze soldier with his head bowed and hands resting on the butt of his rifle, standing on a simple square-section stone plinth mounted on a splayed base. It commemorates the 720 residents of Streatham who lost their lives in the First World War and was rededicated by the Mayor of Wandsworth in May 1959 to also commemorate the dead of the Second World War.

The statue was made by the well-known Birmingham sculptor, Albert Toft, who designed war memorials in his home city, including within the Hall of Memory, and also in Holborn, Oldham, Stone (Staffordshire), Ipswich and Leamington Spa, together with the statue of Queen Victoria in the Memorial Gardens in Nottingham.

In the background of the photograph of c1925 is the United Services Club which occupied "The Chimes", a property which was destroyed during the Blitz in 1944, and replaced by the 1950s Albert Carr Gardens housing estate. The memorial is in the Streatham Common Conservation Area but is currently unlisted.

Stockwell War Memorial - Clapham Road - Grade II

The war memorial in Stockwell is a tower with a clock on all four faces. It was unveiled by Princess Alice, Countess of Athlone, in May 1921 (when this photo top left was taken) in memory of those who lost their lives in the First World War. It was designed by Frank T. Dear in the neo-Grecian style, the 45-foot high tower of Portland stone has a relief figure of Remembrance in Greek mourning dress.

Memorial to Edmund Distim Maddick - West Norwood Cemetery - Grade II

This highly distinctive mausoleum was commissioned by the surgeon and cinematographer Edmund Distim Maddick and completed in 1936, although he did not die until 1939. It is of Portland stone and has a square plan with an unusual tapering stone roof pieced by a tall glazed cruciform-shaped window on each face. It is surmounted by sculptured figures of Jesus and a child. The doorcase and glazed bronze doors leading into the marble-lined chamber are especially fine (photo left).

Brixton Waterworks Pumping Station - Jebb Avenue

Waterworks have occupied this site for over 175 years - the Lambeth Waterworks Company built the reservoirs on the 16-acre site to the north of this pumping station in 1834, together with their headquarters. They soon sold part of their land to Brixton Prison, a private company until taken over by the government in 1853. The Lambeth Waterworks Company was taken over in 1902 by the Metropolitan Water Board, which built this impressive pumping station in c1930. It is designed in the attractive Beaux-Arts George V idiom of red brick with stone cornice and string-course, tall metal windows; those on the bays either side of the projecting central section facing Jebb Avenue having lunette windows with stone keystones. The two massive chimney stacks dominate the composition. These waterworks were built to serve a huge area extending out to Streatham, Norwood, Forest Hill and Selhurst. It is unlisted but has been protected by the designation of the Rush Common and Brixton Hill Conservation Area since 1997.

Telephone box near Lambeth Palace

There are ten Grade II listed telephone boxes in Lambeth, although all but one (on Denmark Hill adjacent to Ruskin Park) are in Kennington and Waterloo. They were designed by Sir Giles Gilbert Scott (consulting architect of the 1930s County Hall North and South Blocks) for the Post Office Telephones department.

Half of Lambeth's listed telephone boxes are of the K2 type designed in 1927 and the others are the K6 types which are slightly smaller and simpler, designed in 1935. The example pictured here is a K6 box on the river frontage near Lambeth Palace and Lambeth Bridge.

Gipsy Hill Telephone Exchange – Rosendale Road

This telephone exchange is a striking 1930s landmark at the junction of Rosendale Road and Park Hall Road. It was designed by Office of Works architect Christopher Bristow. It is unusual for this period as most telephone exchanges were built in the 'Post Office Georgian' style (the telephone system was run by the Post Office until it was privatised in 1981) but the Gipsy Hill exchange is a bold modern style with a dramatic canted tower on the corner and long plain red brick wings extending south and west.

A ceramic plaque high up on east facade records not only the date of construction (1936) but also the royal cipher of the uncrowned King Edward VIII who abdicated in that year. It has no heritage protection.

Other examples of exchanges in Lambeth of this period are the Tulse Hill Exchange off New Park Road and the Kennington Exchange just off Kennington Park Road. The latter dates from c1930 and is a more traditional George V style design in yellow stock brick with tall windows topped with keystones, some carved with the heads of historical figures, and a slate mansard roof with dormers.

Education

Former Brixton School of Building - Ferndale Road

This former college building occupies the site of a public baths opened by the Surrey County Cricket Club in 1874. This venture failed and the site was acquired by the London County Council (LCC) for their Brixton School of Building, which opened in 1904 and soon gained an international reputation for excellence in the fields of town planning, building technology and estate management. The LCC added a school of architecture in 1906, directed until 1928 by the renowned architect Arthur Beresford Pite. Pite designed Christ Church on Brixton Road, St Saviour's Parish Hall in Herne Hill and the Anglican cathedral in Kampala, Uganda. In 1972 the school relocated to South Bank Polytechnic's new Wandsworth Road site (now closed and transferred to South Bank University's Elephant and Castle campus). The buildings then became an adult education centre until it too closed. The 1935 frontage building was saved by its inclusion within the Ferndale Road Conservation Area in 1997 and it was converted into apartments in c2002 with a bold roof extension. The remainder of the old college buildings were demolished and replaced by blocks of flats. The 1935 building was erected in an era of great expansion of further education when large technical colleges were built throughout London. It is a well-proportioned design - three storeys of London stock brick with an imposing central entrance of Portland stone bearing the crest of the LCC and the name of the college in gilded lettering incised into the stone. It is proposed for local listing.

Former Aspen House Open Air School (now Orchard Primary School) - Cotherstone Road - Grade II

This school has a fascinating history, and its charming timber pavilions standing in an orchard setting resemble a colonial school of the British Empire. It was built in 1925 by the London County Council's Architect's Department as an open-air school for children suffering from the then endemic tuberculosis and other conditions such as asthma and anaemia. The school employed a progressive educational curriculum of small classes, physical exercise, nature study, creative play and gardening to build up the strength of the pupils in poor health. The children were given three nourishing meals a day, an hour's rest in the afternoon on day beds in the open air, and lessons in open-sided classrooms to maximise their exposure to sunshine and fresh air. The site was originally occupied by a large villa called Aspen House which was demolished but its stable block was retained and used by the school; it survives to this day.

There are three classroom pavilions with hipped roofs and deep overhanging eaves. The classrooms are raised off the ground on timber posts which support the joists and the floorboards. Each classroom was fully open to the elements above timber waist-high walls when they were first built but were fully enclosed by continuous windows of paired side-hung casements, probably in the 1950s. A fourth, much larger pavilion with rooflights accommodated the dining room, also used for the children's afternoon nap on wet days.

Jessop Primary School - Lowden Road - Herne Hill

Jessop Primary School in Herne Hill was another progressive school design by the LCC from the 1930s. At a time when most schools were being built in a formal 20th century Georgian style with pitched hipped tiled roofs, sash windows and classical trimmings, the flat-roofed modern style Jessop Primary with its huge low-cilled windows represented a new trend in school architecture. It exemplifies the over-riding concern of the 1930s with fresh air and sunshine with a much less formal approach to teaching and encouraging creative play.

The school was opened on 26 April 1938, replacing Jessop Road Infants and Junior schools, Victorian buildings built by the London School Board in 1876, which were by then severely overcrowded. The 1938 building was designed for a roll of 482. It was renamed Jessop Primary School in 1951 and was recently extended in a relatively sympathetic fashion. It has no heritage protection.

Henry Fawcett Primary School - Bowling Green Street - Kennington

Henry Fawcett Primary School was built to serve one of the largest and most ambitious municipal housing estates to be built in Lambeth in the 1930s - the Kennington Park Estate. Both the estate and the school were built by the London County Council Architect's Department - the school dates from c1935 and is very similar in plan, form and design to Jessop Primary. It is orientated so that both its playground and its principal elevation face south to maximise day and sunlight within the classrooms and during playtime breaks.

Particularly fine features of this school are its moderne entrances which have beautifully-crafted brickwork in the Dutch Dudok style and sculptured stone owls.

Henry Fawcett (1833-1884) was a radical academic and liberal MP for Hackney, who lived on South Lambeth Road. He was a very early campaigner for women's right to vote. He was appointed Postmaster General by Gladstone in 1880. It has no heritage protection.

Streatham Hill & Clapham High School - Abbotswood Road

This was the former Battersea Grammar School, relocated from its original site on St John's Hill to this impressive school building built in 1936. It was designed by J.E.K. Harrison on an eight-acre site provided by the LCC who contributed to the £55,000 cost of its construction, also funded by the sale of the original site in Battersea. The three-storey school was designed for 540 pupils and was progressive in its design. It has two long wings with end pavilions and a central double-height assembly hall with large windows. It is of an elegant moderne style which is not dissimilar to the Grade II listed Burlington Danes School in Hammersmith built in the same year, designed by Burnet, Tait & Lorne. Battersea Grammar closed in 1977 but this fine school building avoided the fate of many i.e. demolition, finding an ideal new use as the Streatham Hill and Clapham High School. The beautiful stone eagle with the original name of the school inscribed below still stands at the entrance. The school has been greatly extended but the view of it from the road is little changed. View from playing fields c1950.

Public Health

Former South London Hospital for Women - Clapham Common Southside (now The Latitude apartment building and a Tesco store)

This building is both a success story and a regrettable loss of Lambeth's rich architectural heritage. The frontage was saved from demolition in 1997 and well restored in 2004 with its missing wing completed; however its elegant interiors were destroyed.

This hospital was founded in 1912 by two female surgeons at the Elizabeth Garrett Anderson Hospital in Euston, Eleanor Davies-Colley and Maud Chadburn, who lived and worked together for 25 years. It soon gained a fine reputation for medical care employing only female doctors and treating only women, and children under seven.

The first buildings were opened in 1916 (site A on this plan of 1935) and it was enlarged over the next 40 years. The most impressive building was the frontage block of 1930 designed by one of the 20th century's greatest architects, Sir Edwin Cooper, (sites B and C). This was partly new-build and partly a re-fronting of earlier structures. The cross wings (additional wards) were built between 1935 and 1940 (D). Its southern wing (E) was not built due to a lack of funds leaving the composition lop-sided (this part of the site was occupied by a 19th century house and the 1916 building), but it was finally built in 2004 allowing Cooper's original design to be appreciated in its full glory.

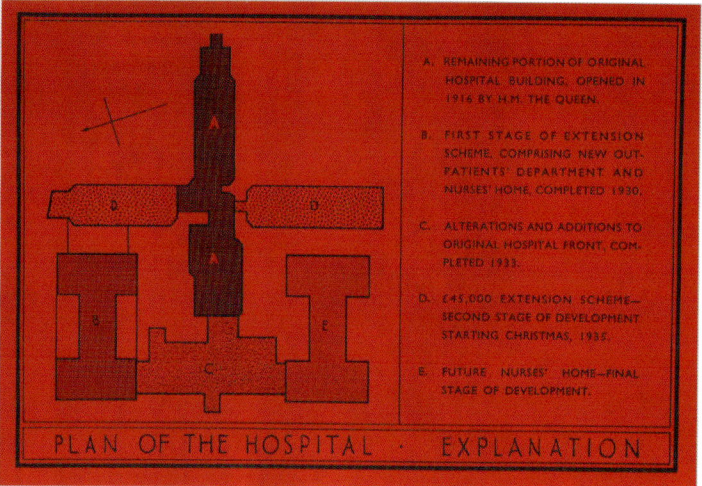

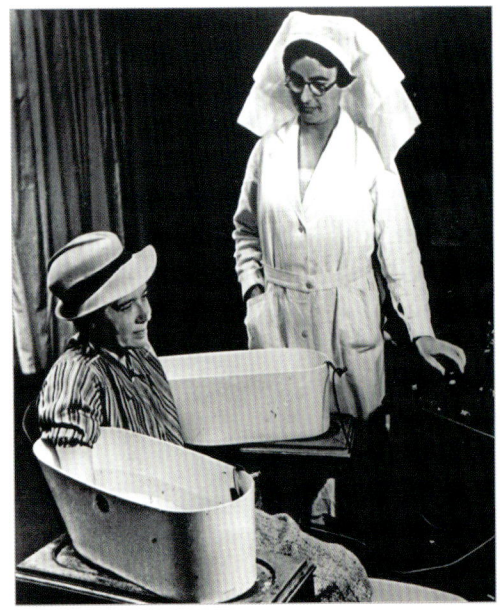

Sir Edwin Cooper designed a dignified neo-classical George V style building with beautiful red brickwork, rusticated at ground-floor level below a broad band of Portland stone, multi-paned sash windows with timber shutters on the upper floors, continuous iron balconies above the second-floor stone cornice and a steep mansard roof with timber pedimented dormers and tall brick chimneys. A ramp enabled ambulances to pull up at the first-floor entrance hall level. It is very similar to Cooper's Devonport House Nurses Home in Greenwich, which also opened in 1930 and is Grade II listed, therefore retaining many of its elegant interiors.

There were some magnificent interiors at the South London Hospital including a panelled boardroom with Adam-style plasterwork ceiling and the imposing barrel-vaulted Outpatients Waiting Hall (both pictured here) together with Georgian-style oak staircases. The photo to left shows a nurse and patient at the hospital in 1935.

The hospital was incorporated into the National Health Service in 1948 but was closed in 1984 despite huge public protest including the occupation of the hospital and a petition signed by 60,000 people. The hospital buildings remained vacant and deteriorating for nearly 20 years. In 1997 Tesco attempted to win permission to raze the whole hospital to the ground and replace it with a tower block of flats and a new store. This plan was strongly contested by Lambeth Council (who had included the site within the Clapham Conservation Area in 1986), local residents and amenity groups, who together won their fight at a major public inquiry in 1998.

Tesco then agreed to retain Cooper's 1930s frontage and in 2004 it was refurbished by leading conservation architect Giles Quarme when the missing pavilion was finally executed (seen in the foreground of this photo to the right), 75 years after the original building was opened, greatly improving the appearance of this landmark. This included the removal of the ambulance entrance ramp and clumsy porch, which was replaced by an elegant flight of steps leading to a bridge to the front door, all with classical balustrades.

Sadly English Heritage declined to list the building so Lambeth was unable to save the fine interiors. The building is now flats with a new residential wing to the rear adjacent to a new Tesco store with a large car park. These new-build structures replaced the remainder of the hospital buildings.

The Guthrie Clinic - King's College Hospital

King's College Hospital on Denmark Hill was opened in 1913 by King George V and Queen Mary. The original buildings were designed by William Pite (elder brother of Arthur Beresford Pite, architect of Christ Chuch Brixton Road of 1907 and Church of St Saviour Herne Hill Road of 1915) accommodating 600 beds in six pavilion ward blocks. In 1937 a new extension to accommodate a wing for private patients was opened, named the Guthrie Clinic, which still performs this function today.

It is a very bold architectural statement - a tall stepped tower of red-brown brick with a recess framed by quarter-section fluted columns above an elaborate urn which stands above the projecting stone-pedimented first-floor central window. The tower has the stepped massing of a New York skyscraper forming a striking landmark on Denmark Hill and fronts a long four-storey wing which extends west into the hospital site. It was designed by Stanley Hamp of architects Colcutt and Hamp. Hamp also designed the huge art deco Adelphi office block on the Victoria Embankment (1938), which is Grade II listed, and several private houses. The Guthrie Clinic is proposed for local listing.

Former Wandsworth War Memorial Maternity Home

Only one building remains of the Weir Hospital on Weir Road, opened in 1913, following its closure in 1977. This is the Maternity Home - a jolly three-storey building with a top storey of red brick and stone stripes, built in 1931, designed by R.J. Thompson. He was a local architect who designed school buildings and a swimming baths in nearby Wimbledon. It has an imposing centre-piece of stone with a segmental arched pediment and porch over the entrance.
The hospital stood empty for years. Despite its inclusion within the La Retraite Conservation Area, designated in 1984, all the attractive Edwardian buildings were cleared by 1986 and replaced by Molly Huggins Close. Only the 1931 building and the Edwardian front boundary railings survived, the building continuing as a day centre for many years. It is proposed for local listing.

Leisure and Entertainment

Streatham Odeon (former Astoria Cinema) - Streatham High Road

This palatial cinema with a capacity of 2,614 was designed by Edward A. Stone and opened on 30th June 1930. Stone was an accomplished cinema and theatre architect who designed four other Astorias in this period: Brixton - now the Academy (1929), Finsbury Park (1930) - both Grade II* listed; Old Kent Road (1930) demolished in 1984 and the Astoria on Charing Cross Road (1927), also, sadly, demolished, in 2010. He also designed the Prince Edward Theatre in Old Compton Street, opened in 1930, a design similar to that of the Streatham Odeon.

The Streatham Astoria is built in brick with a rendered ground floor and a swept pantile roof which has a long central dormer. It is a symmetrical composition, the end bays projecting forward of the seven-bay frontage of entrance doors with double-height windows above. The fourth floor, under the deep eves supported on paired consoles, is of dressed stone with small square windows.

The interior of the auditorium was decorated in the Egyptian style popular at the time. The opening of the Astoria, seen in the upper photo, was a glittering occasion - the 16th Hussars playing a fanfare of trumpets. The Astoria was taken over by the Odeon chain in 1961 and sub-divided in 1979 to create three screens. It lies within the Streatham Hill and Streatham High Road Conservation Area and is also proposed for local listing.

Former Regal/ABC Cinema - Streatham High Road - Front block listed Grade II

The Streatham Regal was opened in 1938 (it was renamed the ABC Cinema in 1960) and was designed by W.R. Glen, who was also the architect for the Regal Camberwell in Southwark, now in church use. The Regal was listed Grade II in 1998 just before the cinema closed in 2000. The listing enabled Lambeth to insist on the retention and restoration of the frontage building and the grand foyer (still awaiting a new use) but the auditorium was demolished in 2004 and replaced by a block of flats named the Picture House.

The curved brick-frontage building has a steel frame clad in brick and a projecting curved faience centrepiece. This has a green mosaic inset, which displayed the film titles, flanked by black glazed pillars. The modern-style brick-banded cornice above resembles that of the Odeon at Swiss Cottage. The strongly vertical staircase tower counterbalances the horizontal emphasis of the double-curved composition. The tall windows on the curving corners have horizontal metal panes and a faience motif at the top.

The double-height foyer (seen in this c1938 photograph) has a pair of graceful art deco dog-leg staircases leading up to the upper foyer where there are two classically inspired medallions which are illustrated on page 6. The stepped ceilings have cornices and friezes. The interior of the lost auditorium was also beautifully decorated with plasterwork, fluted pilasters, niches, ornamental grillwork and a fluted proscenium.

Brixton Academy (former Astoria Cinema) - Stockwell Road - Grade II*

The Brixton Astoria was designed by Edward A. Stone, in 1929, a year before his Streatham Astoria (now Odeon). It is one of Lambeth's most dramatic landmarks. The cream faience-clad facade is dominated by a copper half-dome over the entrance foyer. The grand double-height ocean-liner style foyer is a cacophony of channelled rustication, fluted pilasters, art deco glass light fittings and metal balustrades (see photo below). The auditorium, arguably one of the finest surviving examples of 'atmospheric' cinemas in England (along with the Finsbury Park Astoria), resembles an Italian Renaissance garden,(see 1970 photo below right and next page). Photos date from 1970 and 1974.

The monumental proscenium is topped by an Italian loggia based on the Rialto Bridge in Venice (bottom right photo) running above the arch with a grand central doorcase, balcony and broken pediment. Each side of the arch is a Portmerion-style Mediterranean village of windowed facades, balustrades, baroque pavilions, pediments, statues and artificial trees and climbers. These features were all imaginatively lit and complemented by a domed roof adorned with planets and stars, also illuminated to create a spectacular vision of fantasy.

Like many super-cinemas of this period it was also designed for live performances so has a huge stage with extensive back stage facilities. The luxurious design was facilitated by American money invested in the Astoria chain.

The cinema operated for over forty years, finally succumbing to closure in 1972 when it was proposed for demolition, to be replaced by a petrol station and car showroom. Thankfully it was saved by being listed in 1974 and reopened as a concert venue in 1981, becoming the Brixton Academy in 1983, its use ever since.

Kennington Regal Cinema (now flats) - Kennington Road - Locally Listed

The Kennington Regal stands on a prominent site at the junction of Kennington Road and Black Prince Road. It opened in 1930 and was taken over and renamed the Granada in 1949. It closed after a relatively short life as a cinema in 1961, the last films showing were *Genevieve* starring Kenneth More and Kay Kendal and *Doctor at Large* with Dirk Bogarde, Donald Sinden, Muriel Pavlov and James Robertson Justice.

From 1961 to 1997 it was a Granada (later Gala) Bingo Club but the former cinema was to share the same fate as that of the Streatham Regal. It was included in the Kennington Conservation Area in 1997 which saved the elegant foyer structure with its projecting prow and canopy, but the auditorium was demolished and replaced by a block of flats. This has arguably improved the streetscape of Kennington Road as the huge windowless auditorium presented a rather forbidding face along this frontage. The top photo is from c1965, soon after bingo replaced films. It is locally listed.

The former Regal has good group value with the adjacent 1920s pub, the Black Prince which has a fine black-tiled ground-floor frontage (seen in the background of the bottom photo).

Former Gaumont Palace Cinema/ Megabowl - Streatham Hill

The Gaumont Palace Cinema was designed by Charles Nicholas and J.E. Dixon Spain - the latter was an architect of some note who also designed the Quasr el Aini State Hospital in Cairo, Newcastle City Hall and Baths (Grade II listed), the Rock Hotel in Gibraltar and numerous churches, schools and film studios.

It opened in 1932 (when the top photograph was taken), seating 2,381 patrons, and featured an open air terrace serving the café. This was located beneath the tall loggia supported on fluted columns between the two 'bookend' bays of red brick on rusticated rendered bases.

It was damaged in the blitz and was eventually reopened as simply the Gaumont in 1955, having been remodelled by the architects T.P. Bennett. Its opening film in 1955 was *Doctor At Sea*, starring Dirk Bogarde, Joan Sims and Brigitte Bardot. The cinema use was however short-lived and it closed just six years later in 1961, when the building was converted into a bowling alley. This in turn closed in 2008. It is unlisted but lies within the Streatham Hill & Streatham High Road Conservation Area. There are now plans to demolish the building, retaining the facade which would front a new block of flats.

Granada Cinema (now South Bank Gym) - Wandsworth Road

The Granada opened in 1936 with the film *Queen of Hearts*, starring Gracie Fields, replacing a smaller 1920s cinema, the Clock Tower. The Granada was the only cinema to be designed by Edward Lyons, Laurence Israel and Cecil Elsom, architects of national renown. Lyons and Israel also designed Wolverhampton Civic Hall (1934), several housing developments in Blackheath and Richmond, and the Annex to the Old Vic Theatre on The Cut. They are all Grade II listed but the Granada has no heritage protection.

The Granada has a very stylish modern horizontal emphasis accentuated by the slender bands of white stone which extend to the north facing side elevation and rows of deeply inset windows. The lidded brick tower over the entrance retains its vertical fin sign. The cinema seated over 2,000 in the stalls and balcony. On each side of the proscenium were large panels of coffered squares and decorative motifs depicting musical instruments sculpted by Frank Baines. A magnificent Wurlitzer organ entertained patrons before the film. In common with many variety-cinemas it had a fully equipped stage and dressing rooms. It closed in 1965, the final film being *Carry on Nurse*, and became a Granada Bingo Club which closed in 1977. It was converted to its current use as a gym in 1986.

Streatham Hill Theatre (now Beacon Bingo) - Grade II

The Streatham Hill Theatre, designed by W.G.R. Sprague and W.H. Burton, was opened in 1929 by the actress Evelyn Laye. It has a steel frame construction clad in brick with a facade of Doulton's Carrera terracotta faience. The bookend pavilions have festoons beneath the pediments and are linked by an open parapet recessed behind Tuscan columns. The interiors are magnificent - an imperial stair rises from the opulent lobby to an upper foyer which leads into the grand auditorium decorated with urns, sphinxes and giant Ionic columns. The theatre was once the venue for large production companies such as the D'Oyly Carte Opera Company but closed in 1962 and has since hosted bingo.

Brockwell Lido - Dulwich Road - Herne Hill - Grade II

Brockwell Lido was built by the London County Council in 1931. The pool is enclosed by a three-meter high brick wall with flat-roofed pavilion buildings around the perimeter accommodating the poolside cafe, changing rooms, plant and the entrance hall. The western pavilion has a projecting bay with integral clock. The top left image is of c1938. The octagonal fountain pictured above was removed in the 1970s.

The lido was sympathetically extended to the south by Pollard Thomas Architects in 2004, adding a members' gym and refurbishing the facilities.

The Duke of Sussex - Baylis Road, Waterloo

Eight public houses built in Lambeth between the wars have been selected to demonstrate the great diversity of architectural styles in this period. All are very typical designs of the 1920s and 1930s, found the length and breadth of England, and yet, they could not be more different in their appearance.

The Duke of Sussex was designed by Truman's in-house architectural team in 1924 and is a fusion of the 20th century Georgian genre (witness the sash windows, cornice details, copper-clad dormers and fine brickwork) and lingering Edwardian features from twenty years before - the faience dressings and raised ceramic lettering of a traditional 1900s boozer. It has no heritage protection despite it being an increasingly rare survivor, retaining its individual character and charm in this modern-day age when many others of its ilk have been subject to corporate make-overs, closure for conversion to residential, or demolition.

The Old Red Lion - Kennington Park Road - Grade II

The Old Red Lion is an exuberant example of the 'Tudorbethan' style, popular for pubs and housing in the inter-war years. The frontage is timber-framed with plastered infill recreating the Merrie Olde England style of Tudor-inspired nostalgia.

The two red brick chimney stacks and gabled second-floor centre-piece complete with bargeboards and red lion-shaped brackets enliven the roofscape. The windows are leaded-light casements, continuing the 16th century theme, as does the traditional hanging sign at high level and the brick noggin to the stall-risers below the windows to the bar on the ground-floor.

A single-storey structure to the left is a reminder of the off-licences attached to many pubs during this period. The interior too is remarkably intact and well worth a visit to enjoy its oak-beamed ceiling, Tudor-style fireplaces and original lantern-style lighting.

Prince of Wales (and KFC)
- Coldharbour Lane - Brixton
- Locally Listed

The Prince of Wales is a key landmark at the heart of Brixton facing the Town Hall, St Matthew's Church and the Ritzy Cinema which are all grouped around the recently upgraded central square. It makes the most of its corner site with a superbly confident design resembling the stern of a great ship - its height emphasised by the stepped parapet, the art deco projecting vertical fins striding across the facade and the beautifully crafted end bays of faience surmounted by the Prince of Wales fleur-de-lys.

The pub was designed by architect Joseph Hill and built as part of a 1930s development of shops and banks that extended up to Atlantic Road on land previously protected by the Rush Common legislation. The pub has played an important role in Brixton's social history for over seventy years; it was a gay pub in the early 1980s and was later reduced in size to make way for the current fast-food outlet. The upper floors were recently refurbished and the imaginative Heron weathervane (by local Clapham artist Maggi Hambling) added to the roof, further enhancing the building's landmark presence.

The perspective was produced at the time of its construction in 1938. The building is locally listed and lies within the Brixton Conservation Area.

The Greyhound - Streatham High Road and Greyhound Lane

The Greyhound, rebuilt in 1930 on the site of a much older tavern, is of a composite style. The roofline is clearly influenced by the Elizabethan tradition with a series of gables with decorated bargeboards and lintels over the leaded-light casement windows. Its tall brick chimneys are like those of a manor house of the Tudor period. The projecting single-storey element on Greyhound Lane however is more classical with oeil-de-boeuf (oval) windows and a formal balustrade with art nouveau coping stones. It lies within the Streatham Common Conservation Area but is unlisted.

The former King of Sardinia - Somers Road, Brixton

This jolly pub also dates from c1930 when the previous pub of the same name, which dated back to before 1875, was rebuilt. It closed in 2003 and was recently sensitively converted to residential use as flats after the building had served its community for some seventy years. It is a riot of well-detailed decorative features, most notably the barley-sugar chimneys and columns supporting the projecting first floor. It is protected by the Rush Common and Brixton Hill Conservation Area.

The Horns Tavern - Knights Hill, West Norwood

This is an unusual pub by virtue of its prow-end design and elegant seamed copper roof. It is squeezed onto a narrow triangular site above the railway cutting, opposite West Norwood Railway Station. It has a cheerful red brick upper-floor elevation, and casement windows above which are vertical tiles. The rendered ground-floor frontage is enlivened on the corner above the entrance by a projecting concrete balcony with art deco style railings. The present 1930s pub is on a site occupied by far older hostelries of the same name - John Rocque's map of London of 1745 records the Horns Tavern nearly 300 years ago. This pub has no heritage protection as it lies a few feet outside the West Norwood Conservation Area.

The Plough - Clapham High Street

The Plough on Clapham High Street is another good example of Ye Olde English half-timbered style of the 1920s. Perhaps this was a reaction after the slaughter of the First World War - a desire to return to times past to banish the horrors of the trenches. The original pub was a much older hostelry, dating back to its days as a coaching inn in the 18th century but rebuilt after a fire in 1816. In 1928 the architect Edward A. Stone (architect of the Astoria cinemas in Brixton and Streatham) refronted and extended it on a huge scale rising to four storeys. It has a noble double-height canted oriel bay of leaded-pane windows and three magnificent groups of barley-sugar twist chimneys. The Plough would look equally at home in a Shropshire valley. It lies within the Clapham Conservation Area but is unlisted.

Former Bell Public House - Lambeth Road

The Bell was a Watneys pub which is long since closed but the building remains, opposite Lambeth Palace, little altered. This photograph was taken in 1931, presumably soon after its completion, and shows its charming, very tall and steep pointed gables either side of an even taller chimney stack. It is designed in a romantic picturesque Tudorbethan style – its stone mullions, leaded-light windows and tiled clad hipped-roofed dormers again evoke the Merrie Olde England character. This is reinforced by the jolly figure of a cheeky bell-ringer carved in stone high up on the corner chimney stack. It is now in office and residential use. The Bell was included within the Lambeth Palace Conservation Area in 1997.

Kennington Park Rose Garden - Grade II Registered Park and Garden

Between the wars the London County Council and the metropolitan borough councils invested heavily in improving their parks and open spaces. Ambitious landscaping schemes were regarded as important ways of improving the lives of local communities by encouraging them to enjoy fresh air and attractive public spaces they could be proud of, and also as a means of job creation during the depression years, to boost employment.

The Rookery on the edge of Streatham Common, and Ruskin Park in Herne Hill were earlier LCC projects whose design ethos was developed further at Kennington Park, where a formal Old English rose garden was created. Opened in 1931, complete with a shingle roofed shelter at its eastern end, it featured paths laid with crazypaving, solid timber benches and pergolas supported on stone piers with tile rustication. The photograph below is from 1934.

Inter-war Lambeth on the move

Clapham Common Underground Station - Grade II

This station was opened in 1900 as the southern terminus of the City and South London Railway, extended from Stockwell in that year. It was rebuilt in 1923-24 on the present site (the 1900 station was on the corner of Clapham Park Road and Clapham High Street now occupied by a vent shaft and advert hoardings) to the design of Charles Holden who went on to complete many outstanding underground stations in the 1930s.

Clapham Common station is a modest circular domed building which retains its 1920s UndergrounD motif on a blue frieze around the base of the dome and its internally illuminated roundels mounted on flagpoles with finials.

It is constructed of blocks of structural faience (as opposed to faience cladding) with a black plinth and top moulding. Twin staircases with central cast-iron balustrades lead down to the sub-surface ticket hall.

This is one of only two surviving London Underground stations to retain its central island platform (a single platform with two faces) - the other being the next station at Clapham North. The top photograph is of 1934.

Former LCC Tramways Depot - Brixton Hill

The tram service was extended up Brixton Hill in 1891, cable-drawn at first before being electrified in 1904. In 1922 the London County Council, which had taken over the operation of the tram network in the capital in 1900, built a new depot on Brixton Hill, designed by their architects department headed by George Topham Forrest. It could hold 30 trams and is a simple garage structure with a part-glazed dual-pitched roof supported on brick retaining walls which form the boundary with surrounding properties. Following the withdrawal of trams in 1951 it accommodated motor buses for a few years but closed and found a new use as a Stratstone car showroom. It was however brought back into use as a bus garage in 2004.

Its monumental facade of stock brick decorated with engineering brick patterns has an elegant massing, comprising curving wings accentuating the projecting central bay, where the great arched opening forms the entrance into the depot. A date stone at the top of the arch records its opening in 1922. The original sign 'LCC Tramways' which had decayed during its long period as a car showroom, was reinstated in c2005. The top photograph dates from 1934. It lies within the Rush Common and Brixton Hill Conservation Area and is proposed for local listing.

Lambeth Bridge - Grade II

The present Lambeth Bridge was opened by King George V and Queen Mary in July 1932 (the top photo shows part of the royal opening ceremony). It replaced a suspension bridge built in 1862 which remained a toll bridge until 1879. By 1910 the condition of this bridge had deteriorated to such an extent it was closed to vehicular traffic. The First World War delayed its replacement but parliamentary powers were obtained in 1924. The London County Council commissioned eminent architect Sir Reginald Blomfield to work with their consultant engineer Sir George William Humphreys and their chief architect George Topham Forrest to design the new structure.

It has five-span steel arches supported on reinforced concrete piers and abutments faced with polished Cornish granite. The coat of arms of the LCC is sculpted on the piers and the bridge is lit by its original cast-iron lamp standards mounted on granite uprights or black lattice supports. Pairs of stone obelisks flank each approach, topped by finials – some say these are pine cones (an ancient symbol of hospitality), others say they are pineapples (introduced by botanist John Tradescant who is buried in nearby St Mary's). The red colour of the bridge matches the red seats in the House of Lords, just as the green of Westminster Bridge (opened in 1862) matches the green benches in the House of Commons.

Housing

Public housing

Lambeth, in common with most London boroughs, has an impressive range of inter-war public housing built mainly by the London County Council (LCC) but also by the borough council, housing trusts and other providers such as the Duchy of Cornwall. These typically take the form of estates of varying sizes from the modest to the huge - of blocks of flats in inner London and cottage-estates of semi-detached or short terraces of housing further out in the suburbs (**cottages on Central Hill** in **Norwood** are pictured here).

One charming example of a small housing scheme between the wars is the **Thrale Almshouses** on **Polworth Road** in Streatham (bottom photo). They were designed by architect Cecil M. Quilter and built in 1930, replacing the original almshouses on Streatham High Road which were demolished in the same year to make way for Burton's taylor's shop (featured later in this book). These dated from 1832 and were bequeathed by the three daughters of Henry Thrale (Hester Maria, Susannah Arabella and Cecilia Margaretta) to provide subsidised lodgings for four poor widows or spinsters in their old age. The almshouses are grouped around three sides of a broad quadrangle of lawn and trees. They are designed in a picturesque Georgian tradition with brick elevations articulated by rusticated pilasters, steeply-pitched roofs with tall lead-clad dormer windows and solid chimney stacks. Each home has one bedroom and residents also benefit from a day lounge.

By 1918 the LCC had a proud track record of providing social housing, having built attractive estates at Millbank and Boundary Street in the 1890s and cottage estates such as Totterdown Fields and Norbury in the 1900s. Following the end of the First World War there was a severe housing shortage and the government embarked upon a successful 'Homes Fit For Heroes' campaign. The LCC began an ambitious programme of slum clearance with a target of re-housing some 150,000 Londoners, aided by the 1919 'Addison' Housing Act which subsidised the cost of building council housing with state grants. In the 1920s the main focus was on developing cottage estates on the edge of the capital - on a vast scale such as Becontree, Downham and St Hellier. The Lambeth examples, mostly in Norwood (see top photo on previous page of cottages on Central Hill) are on a smaller scale but in a similar idiom of vernacular style cottages with red pantile roofs, bay windows, timber porches and generous gardens – according with the high standard laid down within the Tudor Walters report of 1918. This set down ideal room sizes, requirements for bathrooms (an unheard of luxury for many) and a low density of 12 houses to the acre. By the late 1920s the LCC turned its attention to clearing the large areas of mainly early 19th century houses in the inner city condemned as slum housing and replacing them with higher density estates of flats. They were aided by the 1930 Housing Act which had imposed a duty on authorities to re-house all those displaced by slum clearance, providing a new state subsidy for council housing. Whereas in the 1920s some 95% of new council housing was on the cottage estates, by 1937 nearly 65% consisted of flats in block dwellings. This was also due to early green belt protection to stop the outward spread of London and competition from private house-builders in the outer suburbs.

In addition there was increasing opposition from owner-occupiers in the leafy outer suburbs to new council housing and a preference of many prospective council tenants to remain in their existing communities. They resented the expensive fares and long commuter journeys to work in inner London's industrial and commercial areas or the docks. One of the finest examples in Lambeth is **China Walk** in Kennington (pictured to left) which was designated a conservation area in 1998.

In 1934 with the election of Herbert Morrison's new Labour administration the LCC programme was accelerated under his slogan "Up with the houses and down with the slums". Over half of the LCC's new estates of flats in the inter-war years were developed in just four of the present-day boroughs- Southwark, Lewisham, Wandsworth and Lambeth (which in 1965 took over large parts of Wandsworth including the vast Springfield Estate) resulting in Lambeth having one of the highest concentrations of the LCC's housing legacy of the inter-war years. Between 1918 and 1940 the LCC built some 6,500 new council homes in Lambeth (based on the boundaries of the present day borough). The LCC's 'house-style' for flats in the 1920s and 30s was a pleasing 20th century Georgian genre of solid brick elevations with regular fenestration of multi-paned sash windows and steeply-pitched tiled roofs. Balconies of iron railings or brickwork accessed short runs of flats from communal staircases lined with tiles. Classic examples in Lambeth are the late 1920s and 30s blocks of the Clapham Park (East), China Walk, Springfield and Kennington Park estates. In the mid 1930s art deco and modern movement influences began to appear with curved Crittall windows and a more horizontal emphasis created by the use of bands of brickwork - evident on estates at Oaklands, Poynders Gardens and Tulse Hill.

Lambeth Council was not a great housing provider between the wars compared with boroughs such as Bermondsey and Finsbury but it did cooperate closely with the LCC's housing programme. However the borough did complete a number of council housing schemes and provided some 900 new dwellings.

These included several attractive cottage estates in the south of the borough in Norwood; Edward House, the Black Prince Estate and the **Opal Street Estate** (pictured) - all three in Kennington - and the Henman Estate on the Wandsworth Road. Unfortunately in the 1970s and 80s Lambeth demolished large parts of the latter three estates; however, some blocks remain to be appreciated today including Isabella House on Opal Street, and Deacon House and Sullivan House on Black Prince Road.

The new flats erected by the LCC, Lambeth Council and other housing providers such as the Duchy of Cornwall, the Guinness Trust, the Peabody Trust and the Ecclesiastical Commissioners (later the Church Commissioners) set high standards of design which represented a great improvement in the housing conditions of the poorer classes in Lambeth. The architects sought to maximise the amount of sunlight and ventilation, with landscaped space for children to play, adequate laundry facilities, the latest cooking and heating technology such as gas water heaters and central heating, and new amenities such as shops and new schools. Images of the new flats on **Wootton Street**, Waterloo built by the Ecclesiastical Commissioners in 1938 are shown below, (the photos below were taken soon after its completion). In 1937 the LCC summed up its approach to council housing as *'maintaining an appearance of domesticity whilst keeping within the bounds of economy'*.

Eight examples of inter-war council estates in Lambeth are discussed here.

China Walk in Kennington was one of the LCC's finest estate in this era. It comprises six five-storey blocks of 238 flats covering five acres, built between 1928 and 1934 (when this aerial view was taken). The blocks were named after famous china-ware: Derby, Wedgwood, Worcester, Coalport, Minton and Devonport, reflecting the local ceramic industry, most notably Doulton's at Vauxhall. The estate includes spacious quadrangles of lawns and trees (the principle one is pictured middle left). It is also carefully planned to respect the 18th century building line along Kennington Road and Walnut Tree Walk, employing a dignified 20th century Georgian style of sash windows, brick facades and tiled beehive mansard roofs to blend in with its historic neighbours.

The **Kennington Park Estate** was built after the LCC purchased a huge 18-acre site from the Duchy of Cornwall in 1933, laying out 15 five-storey blocks named after famous cricketers (Blythe, Grace, Reid etc) between 1934 and 1938. It includes the long crescent of flats which form a backdrop to the Oval cricket ground and a very imposing range facing Kennington Park, with stout chimneys and a pleasing rhythm of sash-windows, further articulated by a decorated brick parapet and occasional bay windows. The estate included the Henry Fawcett Junior School (q.v.), a welfare centre, workshops and 16 shops. This estate is pictured in the middle right and bottom views.

The Oaklands Estate on **Poynders Road** in Clapham is a highly distinctive design, recognised in 1999 when it was designated a conservation area. It is a three-acre site comprising three blocks of five storeys providing 185 flats. It was completed by the LCC in 1936 and represents a significant change in their design from the conventional George V style of sash windows and pitched roofs.

Oaklands is a bold display of the 1930s continental moderne genre – flat-roofed, with sweeping, curving balconies in the streamlined ocean-liner style, horizontal alternating bands of coloured brickwork and wide steel-framed Crittall windows to maximise sunlight within (pictured top left).

Clapham Park (East) Estate on **Atkins Road** is a well-planned LCC design of 20 George V style blocks built on a site of 15 acres between 1930 and 1936 decorated with occasional pedimented windows and iron balconies, laid out amongst lawns (pictured below left). **The Kennings Estate** on **White Hart Street** in Kennington was built between 1927 and 1929 to accommodate over 700 residents in 169 flats within seven blocks named after the manors of the Duchy of Cornwall (Fowey, Helston, Liskeard etc). The attractive four and five-storey blocks are in the traditional LCC idiom of stock brick elevations enlivened with red brick quoins, keystones above the tall sash windows and charming beehive mansard roofs (photograph below).

The **Vauxhall Gardens Estate** is one of the most architecturally diverse of the LCC estates in Lambeth and one of the largest, comprising 13 blocks built between 1936 and 1940. The blocks on Glasshouse Walk and Tyers Street have graceful Odeon-style curved corners, horizontal bands of contrasting brickwork, cream-painted rendered canted oriel bay windows and flat roofs concealed by brick parapets (pictured top). The whole estate was designated a conservation area in 2001.

There are several **cottage estates in the vicinity of Norwood Park** that were built by Lambeth Metropolitan Borough Council in the 1920s. These include picturesque vernacular terraces and semi-detached homes on the tree-lined Tivoli Road and Furneux Avenue with their simple rendered elevations, steeply-pitched tiled roofs and overhanging eaves, tile quoins and country cottage porches.

On the eastern edge of the park is the large **Bloomfield cottage estate** completed in 1924. Houses are grouped around a small village green on Durning Road (middle view) or in cul-de-sacs with small greens such as Gibbs Square, graced with bright orange-red tiled cat-slide roofs, pebble-dash elevations and arts and crafts style porches supported on elongated brackets. Cottages with grand classical porches, set back behind privet-hedged front gardens and generous rear gardens, can also be found on nearby **St Gothard Road and St Cloud Road**.

Streatham Hill Estate on **Mountearl Gardens** in Streatham Hill is another notable 1920s estate which comprises small three-storey blocks of flats with unassuming arched entrances, the second floor accommodated within large half-hipped red-tiled mansards. They are grouped in short closes or along curving roads amidst wide expanses of lawns and trees (bottom view).

Duchy of Cornwall Housing

The Duchy of Cornwall continued to develop their Kennington estate, begun in 1913, throughout the 1920s and 30s.

Kennington Palace Court on **Sancroft Street** (top view) is a distinguished Grade II listed apartment building of 1925. Its three wings have modillion cornices, hipped pantile roofs and a Doric porch fronting a lawned quadrangle enclosed by tall railings and ornate gates with pineapple finials on the piers.

Newquay House on **Newburn Street** is a Grade II listed block built in 1934 by Louis de Soissons who designed Welwyn Garden City. It has a central courtyard and tall rounded mansard with wide flat dormers, canted bay windows, rows of Venetian windows, diaper brickwork and the Prince of Wales fleur-de-lys. Photos to left (c1934) and below: left and middle.

60 Sancroft Street is an unusual block of inter-war flats, having traditional three-storey 20th century Georgian elevations of stock brick and sash windows but with a very tall steeply-pitched hipped pantile roof accommodating two additional storeys with two rows of dormer windows (photo below right). It is locally listed and in a conservation area.

Three similar blocks of flats built by the Duchy between 1935 and 1938 are of a similar very high architectural quality – **Tamar House** and **Boyton House** on **Kennington Lane** and **Restormel House** (pictured left) on **Chester Way** are all locally listed. They were all designed by Louis de Soissons in a well-mannered and superbly-detailed George V style.

All are three or four storeys in height and of a very human scale in keeping with the late 18th and early 19th century townscape in the vicinity. They are of yellow stock brick with tiled mansard roofs, simple canted bays of sash windows and elegant stone Gibbs surrounds to their doorways (photo bottom left).

Nos.13-27 Black Prince Road is a charming terrace of eight cottages dating from c1930 which are locally listed and also in a simple Georgian vernacular with dual-pitched plain tile roof between the book-end pavilions projecting towards the street and mainly six-over-six sash windows (photo below).

Other social housing

Two very progressive housing estates were built in the borough by the talented modernist New Zealand architect Edward Armstrong who had practised with the renowned Burnet, Tait & Lorne. His **Loughborough Park Estate** near **Brixton** was built for the Guinness Trust in 1938. It features a striking T-plan community hall (photo right) with integral clock and 1930s stylised lettering, very much in the Dudok tradition. English Heritage refused to list this outstanding building in 2008, which astonished many. The five-storey blocks of flats in matching brown brick are grouped around the hall, set within landscaped areas creating a very pleasing setting. Regrettably however the lack of heritage protection has resulted in its impending demolition and redevelopment.

Armstrong's second estate in Lambeth from the same era is on **Wootton Street** in **Waterloo**, built in 1938 by the Ecclesiastical Commissioners (the forerunner of the Church Commissioners). It also includes a community hall though this has sadly been derelict for some time. It has a nautical feel - long balconies like the decks of an ocean liner and circular port-hole windows together with full-height stair-tower windows extending five storeys. Tait House (photo to right) is particularly fine, a great curved edifice with elongated U-shaped balconies, separated by Octavia Hill Gardens from Benson House. This estate too has no heritage protection.

The elegant **Larkhall Estate** in **Clapham** is one of Lambeth's largest listed buildings (Grade II) comprising 16 five-storey blocks of flats arranged around five generous linked garden quadrangles. It has provided social housing since 1941 but was originally built as a private estate with funding from the LCC.

The first phase was opened in 1929 by the Housing Minister, later to become Prime Minister, Sir Neville Chamberlain. The development, completed in 1931, was commissioned by Sir Theodore Chambers, who was developing Welwyn Garden City at the same time and was a champion of constructing well-built new homes in carefully planned and landscaped surroundings.

The estate was designed by the architects George Grey Wornum (who designed the Royal Institute of British Architects HQ in Portland Place in 1934) and Louis de Soissons who was chief architect to both Welwyn Garden City and the Duchy of Cornwall. It was designed to house 4,500 tenants, replacing housing of a far lower density of some 1,600 whilst at the same time laying out generous landscaped spaces.

It contained a mix of both flats and maisonettes, nearly all of which had their own front door at ground level or on a balcony, some flats having roof gardens. The Larkhall is of a dignified Georgian style akin to the Inns of Court or an Oxbridge college. It retains a wealth of original features such as the cherubs over the doorways, lead-clad porches, picturesque 'Serliana' sashes with Gothik tracery, weatherboard spandrels to the bay windows and Gibbs surrounds to doorways.

Private housing developments

Dumbarton Court on **Brixton Hill** and **New Park Road** (pictured below) is a striking contrast to Larkhall. By 1939 when it was completed, the George V style was increasingly being challenged by the influence of the Modern Movement which was enthusiastically embraced here by its architects Couch & Coupland. It is a bold moderne style with an elegant horizontal emphasis created by the bands of contrasting brown and yellow brickwork, long white rendered balconies and the wrap-around Crittall windows.

It is set around an irregular courtyard and boasts a purpose-built underground garage for 50 cars - highly unusual in 1939, and an air-raid shelter built as the dark clouds of the Second World War were gathering. It was sold to Lambeth Council in 1959. It is proposed for local listing and in common with Christchurch House is protected by the Rush Common and Brixton Hill Conservation Area.

Christchurch House stands at the top of **Brixton Hill** on the South Circular. It was also designed by Couch and Coupland and built in 1938-39. It has a grand double-height entrance portal and highly distinctive projecting balconies with semi-circular prow ends (see photo below). The same horizontal emphasis is reinforced by the bands of concrete between the floors and deep lidded-box eaves. To the rear is a courtyard of landscaped gardens.

Tudor Close is sited half way up **Brixton Hill** and is proposed for local listing. This commanding brick and half-timbered Tudorbethan frontage is set well back behind the protected Rush Common land, now a front lawn to the flats (top image). It was constructed in 1933 and designed by architect A.W. Reading. The developer was Alderman Sir George Broadbridge, who became Lord Mayor of London in 1936, and Member of Parliament for the City of London in 1938 and was later created a Baron. It is also protected by the Rush Common and Brixton Hill Conservation Area. It still has its original swimming pool within the central courtyard.

Pullman Court on **Streatham Hill** is listed Grade II* by virtue of its very progressive white-painted modernist design with a reinforced concrete frame. It is one of the earliest works of its well-known architect Sir Frederick Gibberd who was the principal architect and town planner for Harlow new town, the Catholic Cathedral in Liverpool and the first terminals at Heathrow Airport.

Pullman Court was completed in 1935, comprising 218 flats in three-, five-,and seven-storey blocks on a three-acre site which included landscaped gardens and a swimming pool. The flats were marketed as labour-saving homes for young professional couples. The flats were set well-back from Streatham Hill to preserve a fine group of existing mature trees and have elegant concrete balconies with slender steel balustrading in the constructivist manner. (see lower two photographs, the bottom view is of c1935)

Apartment buildings on Streatham Hill and Streatham High Road

There are so many fine apartment buildings of the 1920s and 30s in Streatham that only a small number can be featured here and they are comprehensively covered in the Streatham Society's excellent book *'The High Road Streatham - an Architectural Appreciation'* by Graham Gower. Here are some of the highlights of this two-mile procession of stately inter-war architecture - none are listed but all lie within this conservation area. **The High** is a gigantic complex of over 170 flats built by R. Toms & Partners for the Bell Property Trust in 1937 (right photo).

Wavertree Court (1933) is seen in the photo middle right. It comprises four-storey blocks with Dutch-style gables, facing onto two central gardens. It was designed by architect Frank Harrington. **Leigham Hall** (photo below left) is another Toms design, built in c1936 and featuring green glazed pantiles and stylish art deco entrances with gilded gazelles.
Streatleigh Court (photo below right) was also designed by Harrington and completed in 1937. This monumental block presides over a busy junction and is dominated by its attractive 'eyebrow'- style balconies and the prow-end of the former Gas Board showroom on the ground-floor.

Telford Court on **Streatham Hill** (photo to right), is a third project by Frank Harrington, demonstrating his versatility in creating very different architectural designs. The front elevation of this long block is articulated by brick balconies at second-floor level, a regular rhythm of set-backs above the shops and charming roof top belvederes. It is interesting to compare this late 1920s design (completed in 1933) which still reflects the popular 20th century Georgian style, with the more moderne and art deco-influenced flats by Harrington and others built just a few years later in the mid 1930s.

Manor Court on **Leigham Avenue** (photo to right) is another Bells development designed by R. Toms. It is very similar to his Ealing Village estate in West London of 1934, which was listed Grade II in 1991. Set around a generous communal garden, Manor Court dates from c1935 and has marvellous art deco-inspired entrance bays with double-height windows to the stairway within. It was provided with a residential club offering dances and other entertainment.

Benshurst Court (photo to right) stands at the southern end of **Leigham Court Road** close to Streatham Common, built on land that once formed part of Sir Henry Tate's adjacent Park Hill estate. It is another American-style apartment development of great character, exhibiting a fusion of modernist and art deco styles. This is particularly evident in the stepped parapets, the vertical fins to the central bays, Crittall windows, ribbed brickwork to the projecting balconies and horizontal-striped facades of alternating brick and render. It was built in c1935 and comprises three three-storey blocks of 24 flats set within landscaped gardens. It included garages reflecting the rising car ownership during this decade. It lies within the Streatham Common Conservation Area.

Trinity Close on **The Pavement - Clapham** was designed by J.J. de Segrais and completed in 1936. It is a suave moderne style apartment building of five storeys - its curvaceous form responds to the diverse townscape of Clapham's Old Town. It is set back behind an 'in-out' driveway with an attractively landscaped front garden and has a rusticated entrance and simple concrete canopy. It is protected by the Clapham Conservation Area but is unlisted (picture left).

Dorchester Court on **Herne Hill** dates from 1934. It is a Grade II listed complex of 96 flats in eight blocks arranged around a broad central garden lit by concrete lamp columns. It is of a sophisticated moderne style in red brick with flat roofs. The strong horizontal emphasis of the long brick balconies is counter-balanced by the vertical elements - the full-height staircase windows above the entrance doors and bookends which frame the approach from Herne Hill and Dorchester Drive at each end of the estate. It was designed by Kemp and Tasker, who also specialised in cinema architecture. Part of the Herne Hill frontage is pictured below left and, below right, the blocks are seen wrapping around the gardens.

Private houses in Clapham, Herne Hill and Streatham

By 1914 almost all of the open land within Lambeth and the districts of Streatham and Clapham which subsequently became part of the borough had been built over. However a few pockets of undeveloped land did remain and these sites, together with the plots of large 19th century houses that were demolished, were developed in the inter-war years. This development mainly took the form of local authority cottage estates or private housing developments often built by small builders.

They reflect the variety of architectural fashions of the 1920s and 1930s, though most are traditional tiled-roof semi-detached homes with bay windows, their spandrels clad in red tiles, smooth or pebble-dash render or weatherboarding. They were usually set back behind modest front gardens, sometimes with room for a short drive and small garage. There are also examples of modernist and art deco designs incorporating large areas of white render and metal-framed Crittall windows. An example in Clapham can be seen to the left and below is a colour-wash perspective of a house in Herne Hill, which survives to this day.

Examples of private houses built between the wars in Streatham and Herne Hill are shown here. They demonstrate the high quality of design and materials, as well as the diversity of styles from the fusion of art deco, modernist and Georgian traditions (evident in the two photos below) to the more vernacular and mid-20th century Georgian: hipped roofs, sash or casement windows and facades of render, hanging tiles or brick (top right, middle right and bottom right photos of houses near Tooting Common in Streatham).

House in Herne Hill - Grade II

This property is one of the finest private houses built in South London in the 1930s. It was designed by architects, Leslie Kemp and Frederick Tasker and was completed in 1936 for a wealthy local businessman who was in the building and development industry.

The house is moderne in style with elevations of mottled red and brown brick laid in a Flemish bond, flat roofs above tiled eaves and tall brick chimney stacks. The casement windows have horizontal glazing bars - contrasting with the sash windows of Edwardian houses just thirty years before and the leaded-light Tudor-style windows or square multi-paned 20th century Georgian design which were both popular ten years earlier, in the 1920s. It is rectangular in plan, complete with an integral garage - a 'must have' for the middle classes by the mid-1930s, together with a billiard room.

The lavishly-appointed art deco interiors include a double-height entrance and stairway hall with very ornate balustrades, and an onyx-lined bathroom.

The house was recently meticulously restored by architects MRJ Rundell & Associates.

Ecclesiastical architecture

Church of the Holy Redeemer - Streatham Vale

The Church of the Holy Redeemer is the parish church of Streatham Vale. It was commissioned by the Church of England to commemorate the work of William Wilberforce, the anti-slavery campaigner. The adjacent church hall dates from 1928 and was designed by Sir Charles Nicholson. The foundation stone of the church was laid in 1931 and it was consecrated on 5th March 1932. It was designed by Martin Travers and M.W. Grant who exhibited drawings of the interior at the Royal Academy in 1933. The church cost £11,775 - a considerable sum at the time. It is built of stock bricks with pre-cast stone tracery in a modified 15th century style. The chancel is a continuation of the nave and the roof is of steel, clad in copper, surmounted by a neo-classical cupola which makes it a striking landmark from afar. It has no heritage protection.

St Anselm's Church - Kennington Road - Grade II

St Anselm's was opened in 1932, designed by leading architects Professor Stanley Adshead and Stanley Ramsey, who had together planned and designed the adjoining Duchy of Cornwall Estate in the 1910s for the Prince of Wales, briefly to become King Edward VIII in 1936. It is a substantial basilica, quite austere on the exterior - simple yellow stock brick elevations and round-headed windows with a circular window at the west end facing Kennington Road. The facade is adorned by an elaborate stone doorcase. The interior has arcades with round arches, a side chapel and a Baldacchino (canopy) over the high altar, which is unusual for an Anglican church. The bottom right view dates from 1933 and also shows the adjoining vicarage built earlier in 1914.

St Bede's Church for the Deaf - Clapham Road - Locally Listed

St Bede's was designed by Sir Edward Maufe - one of two churches built by Maufe for worshippers who were deaf, both opened in 1924. The other is St Saviour's in Acton which is very similar and is Grade II listed (it is an anomaly that St Bede's is unlisted). St Bede's is elevated above a pre-existing structure, an earlier institute and social club for the deaf, again the same scenario as St Saviour's.

The church is in a stylised Gothic idiom incorporating a range of special facilities for the deaf such as a raked floor allowing the congregation much better visibility towards the celebrant and a second pulpit for a sign language interpreter. Either side of the chancel are extensions housing the vestry and a side chapel. The church is incredibly well-detailed reflecting Maufe's great skill in this regard. The hanging star light fittings (matching St Saviour's) are of particular note. It is locally listed and lies within the Clapham Road Conservation Area.

Commercial architecture

Former Woolworth store - Nos.457-461 Brixton Road

F.W. Woolworth built one of their finest art deco store frontages in South London - it stands proudly at the heart of Brixton. It is a glorious essay of cream faience contrasting with the predominantly red brick Victorian and inter-war banks and shopping parades on this stretch of Brixton Road. The facade has a strong vertical emphasis created by the double square-section piers at each end and the fins dividing the tall strips of Crittall windows to the first and second floors. Sadly the individual internally illuminated lettering proclaiming the store's name was removed after Woolworth's closed at the end of 2009 but its shopfront remains in part. The building is now occupied by an H&M store and is protected by the Brixton Conservation Area, but is unlisted.

Sunlight Laundry - No.125 Acre Lane

Another art deco classic has graced Acre Lane on the eastern side of Brixton for over 70 years – the Miami-style range of smooth white render and Crittall windows has a central tower with a tall Cape-Dutch style window between two curving bays above a shallow projecting canopy over the main entrance. It was constructed in 1937, designed by architect F.E. Simpkins who also built the Grade II listed Curry's warehouse and offices at 991 Great West Road in Hounslow. The Sunlight Laundry is not only still in its original use as offices fronting a working laundry behind, but is still in its original ownership - a very unusual scenario for an inter-war building in the 21st century. It is proposed for local listing.

Brixton Markets - Grade II

Brixton has three great market buildings - the smallest is the narrow Reliance Arcade of 1925 which has a stunning art deco Egyptian-style frontage of buff faience and bright primary colours on Electric Lane (see inside back cover).

Market Row is much larger. Opened in 1928 it has three entrances and a broad T-plan. The glazed roof is supported on reinforced concrete open-arched trusses with roundels on the divisions of the retail units (see photo to right).

Finally the Granville Arcade (now renamed Brixton Village) occupies a trapezoidal site with a principal facade on Coldharbour Lane incorporated with a four-storey block of flats called Granville House. The names of the six arcades have an American flavour - First to Sixth Avenue. This was built in 1935-38. From the 1950s they have been popular with the Afro-Caribbean community. All three market halls were listed in 2010 as a result of a concerted local campaign (see inside front cover).

Ivor House - Acre Lane

This is the former South Suburban Co-operative Department store, an imposing four-storey Beaux-Arts style building designed by Frank Bethell in 1928. It offered a series of separate stores including a grocery, hosiery, drapery and outfitters. It has a central bay over the main entrance with a third-floor Diocletian window, concave corner facing the town hall and a prominent mansard roof with a ridge decorated by bundles of rods in the Ionic style, a popular classical reference at this time. It has been used as council offices since the store closed in 1968. It is in the Brixton Conservation Area and is locally listed.

Former Quin & Axten store Nos. 422-438 Brixton Road

This was a large drapers and furnishings store on Brixton Road, stretching from Stockwell Road to Ferndale Road. It was founded in the 1880s but rebuilt in a grand manner in c1930. The photograph of 1934 shows eager shoppers on the first day of the sales - note the large plate glass display windows and stylish floor tiles.

It was bombed in 1941 and rebuilt internally in 1950, but its elegant facades of faience dominated by the monumental central bay with fluted columns and flattened pediment survived together with the dentil cornices and windows with decorated spandrel panels, all well-preserved today.

It was owned for a short period by John Lewis, but in 1950 it was converted into smaller retail units with government offices on the upper floors. It is locally listed.

Former Burton's, now Pratts & Payne Nos. 103-105 Streatham High Road

Montague Burton was the most successful nationwide tailors and gentlemen's outfitters of the 20th century. Stanley Burton and Barbara Jessie, son and daughter of Sir Montague Burton, opened this store in 1932, a ceremony which is commemorated to this day on two plaques. The elaborate 'jazz modern' facade is decorated with stylised elephant heads and art deco motifs - very much the Burton's house style, designed by Harry Wilson, an architect of The Roundhay in Leeds. His Burton's stores in York and Tottenham Court Road are listed Grade II but this Streatham branch is unlisted, though it is protected by the Streatham Hill and Streatham High Road Conservation Area.

South London Press Building - Nos 2-4 Leigham Court Road

Both local and national newspapers enjoyed a period of great expansion between the wars and many built new head offices - the great Fleet Street palaces of the Daily Telegraph and the Express are well known. The South London Press occupies an American style five-storey edifice built between 1935 and 1939, with an early 1960s extension attached to the east. The full-height stairway is housed in a tower which projects above the parapet creating a noble vertical element contrasting with the horizontal strips of windows to the office wings either side. The ground floor is clad in black glazed tiles. This building is also unlisted but lies within the Streatham Hill and Streatham High Road Conservation Area.

Century House - Streatham High Road

This was the purpose-built headquarters of jewellers and goldsmiths James Walker and Sanders & Sons, opened in 1938 and was converted to flats in the 1980s. The impressive stone-clad stair tower with vertical steel-framed windows and giant clock rises above the main entrance and plinth of glazed black tiles. The five-storey block is of horizontal bands of red brick with a mansard and dormers. It is in the Streatham Hill and Streatham High Road Conservation Area but is unlisted.

Maritime House - Clapham Old Town

This headquarters of the National Union of Seamen (now the RMT) has a dignified civic architectural quality - a bold 20th century Georgian design dominated by its central tower with giant carved dolphins and a ship's prow by sculptor P.G. Bentham. The entrance is approached by stone steps with columns below a stone balustrade and Venetian window at the first floor. The unlisted building was designed by L.A. Culliford & Partners and opened in 1939. It contains union offices and flats with an employment exchange in part of the ground floor and an additional floor within a mansard (photo below). It is in the Clapham Conservation Area.

Former David Greig's Head Offices - Nos 133-155 Waterloo Road

All that remains of the imposing head office of the David Greig grocery firm is the opulent stonework of its facade, the remainder was destroyed in the 1980s. Designed by architects Payne and Wyatt it was completed in 1928 (photo below of 1931). Its monumental classical frontage of ashlar stone is divided by Ionic half columns above the ground-floor plinth, and is topped by a modillioned cornice and balustrade parapet.

Between the columns and within the windows with stone book-ends were ornamental metal decorated spandrel panels but these were replaced by smoked dark curtain wall glazing beloved in the 1970s and early 80s. It was listed Grade II 1980 but this did not prevent the gutting of the building soon after.

George West House - Nos 2-3 Clapham Common Northside

This Clapham landmark has a fascinating history - it was built during the First World War and completed in 1916 for Ross Ensign Ltd. This company manufactured lenses and optical equipment such as binoculars, periscopes and survey instruments and so was vital for the war effort. The firm closed in 1975 and it is now the offices of Experian software and data services.

Designed by Searle and Searle, it is a steel-framed four-storey structure with an imposing facade of two-tone red brick, polygonal engaged columns and a dentil cornice, all dominated by the integral clock mounted within a grand stone baroque-style gable. It is unlisted but lies within the Clapham Conservation Area.

Three buildings in Waterloo occupied by Kings College London

Kings College now occupies three former office buildings which span the entire 1914 to 1939 period. The oldest is the **Franklin-Wilkins Building** (photo to right) on Stamford Street which, before its conversion to university use in 1999, was Cornwall House. It was designed by R. Allison and completed in 1915 for His Majesty's Stationery Office. During the First World War it was the King George's Military Hospital which treated over 71,000 patients. It is of robust fireproof iron and concrete construction and was incredibly modern for its day.

No. 127 Stamford Street (photo to right) was a WH Smith printing works; built in 1915 and designed by C. Stanley Peach who also designed the interior of the Grade I listed Haymarket Theatre in 1904 and the 1903 London Bridge Hospital (Grade II) on Tooley Street, Southwark. The stylised WHS logos are still extant within the elaborate Egyptian-style cornice. It has a strong vertical emphasis accentuated by its long strips of windows and the boldly modelled book-end bays. It is now student flats with a gym.

Finally, **The James Clerk Maxwell Building** (bottom photo), formerly known as Waterloo Bridge House is a striking nine-storey building that stands in a commanding position opposite Waterloo Station on the corner of **Waterloo Road** and Stamford Street. It was built in 1938 and has a stone ground-floor elevation with brick faced upper floors articulated by brick pilasters, stepping back at the top levels. The adjoining **No. 137 Stamford Street** (BPP Law School) was designed by George Lansdown Brown in 1932.

Lost Buildings of inter-war Lambeth

Lambeth Bridge House, WH Smith's and Doulton House - Albert Embankment

Lambeth Bridge House

Lambeth Bridge House (pictured right and in the extreme left of the top view of all three buildings) was built in 1938 by Costain's as the headquarters of the Office of Works (which became the Ministry of Works in 1940 and the Department of the Environment in 1970). It was the largest office building in Europe at the time of its construction. It was known as 'London's only Stalinist office block' and was a giant landmark facing Lambeth Bridge for over 60 years until its demolition in 2000 when it was replaced by Parliament View - a block of luxury riverside apartments.

Bridge House – WH Smith's Bookbinding works and Stationery Department

Bridge House was built in 1933 to house WH Smith & Sons' Bookbinding Works and Stationery Department. The firm had been established in 1848 with a bookstall at Euston Station. From 1956 the Book Department also occupied Bridge House, relocating from Strand House, Portugal Street near the Aldwych. In 1967 the centre of book and stationery distribution was moved out to Swindon. It was a superb example of art deco architecture but this style was not widely appreciated in the 1970s when its redevelopment was proposed. It was demolished in c1976 to make way for the International Maritime Organisation building, completed between 1977 and 1982.

This photograph (right) taken shortly after completion in the mid 1930s shows its slender clock tower and strong vertical proportions. It is likely that had this building and Doulton House survived into the 1990s they would have been listed given their special architectural interest as bold art deco designs.

Doulton House

The headquarters of the Doulton ceramics firm was adjacent to WH Smith. This art deco building was designed by T.P. Bennett in 1939. Its facade had four fluted pilasters of gold Carrera-ware surmounted by a 50-foot relief in black, gold and ivory-coloured stoneware by Gilbert Bayes depicting the history of pottery through the ages. The building was sadly demolished in 1978 but the frieze was saved and can be enjoyed today in the Victoria & Albert Museum. This interior view is of the entrance hall in 1953.

Empress Theatre - Brighton Terrace - Brixton

Opened in 1898, this theatre on the corner of Brighton Terrace and Bernay's Grove offered seating capacity of 1,260. It was given an art deco facelift in 1931 when it was reconstructed to increase its capacity to 2,000 patrons and given a striking tall corner tower.

The theatre survived on the variety circuit into the 1950s, renowned for its pantomimes and attracting stars such as Tony Hancock, Max Miller, Stan Laurel and Oliver Hardy. However it struggled to compete with the rapid rise in the popularity of television and it closed to become a Granada Cinema in 1957.

This use only lasted until the late 1960s when it was converted into a bingo hall (when this photograph was taken), before ending up as a furniture storage depot. It was demolished in 1992 and replaced by a utilitarian block of flats.

Regal Cinema - Norwood Road - West Norwood

The Regal Cinema at No. 304 Norwood Road was designed by architect F. Edward Jones in the classical style with a giant arched central window. This stunning art deco cinema, equipped with a three-manual Christie Manual organ (destroyed by a fire following an air-raid), was opened on 16th January 1930 with 2010 seats. Taken over by Gaumont Super Cinemas in October 1935, it closed on 1st February 1964 – the last films being a Peter Seller's double bill of *"I'm Alright Jack"* and *"Two Way Stretch"*.

It reopened as a Top Rank Bingo Club from 20th February 1964 and closed in 1978. It was demolished in 1981 to be replaced by the current B&Q DIY store.

An ornate lamp composed of glass panels set into a painted gold metal frame that used to hang over the main staircase was salvaged during the demolition and now forms part of the Museum of London's collection.

Orange Coach Station - Effra Road - Brixton

Pictured here in 1936, and built in 1927, this was the first motor-coach station in the county of London. Its vehicles carried the Royal crest, being suppliers of coaches to the royal household. The company was acquired by Grey-Green Coaches in 1953 and remained as a subsidiary until 1975 when it finally wound up its operations.

The garage was demolished and today part of the landscaped public open space, Windrush Square, occupies this site.

Waterloo Station Signal Box

Waterloo Signal Box opened in 1936 and stood proudly at the approach to this great railway terminus for over half a century. It was designed in the latest Modern Movement style, in concrete with a projecting lidded flat roof. It was equipped with a Westinghouse power lever frame as the final part of the signalling modernisation project which replaced old semaphore signals with colour light signals. The signal box was closed in 1990 and demolished to enable the construction of the Eurostar terminal which operated between 1994 and 2007 when its services were transferred to St Pancras International.

Morley College & The Ravilious murals – Westminster Bridge Road

The mural by Eric Ravilious (1903-42) was in the Florence Acton Refreshment Room at Morley College, on Westminster Bridge Road. This detail shows George Peele's 'Arraignment of Paris'. The mural was part of a scheme for artists commissioned by the College Principal, Mrs Eva Hubback, with advice from Sir John Rothenstein. Funding of £1,300 was received in 1928 from Sir Joseph Duveen for murals and Ravilious was commissioned, along with Edward Bawden and Cyril [Charles] Mahoney, to paint the public spaces at the college. The official unveiling was by the Prime Minister, Stanley Baldwin, in 1930. They became some of the most influential British murals of the time, but were unfortunately destroyed by bombing in 1940.

Locarno Dance Hall - Streatham Hill

Built in 1929 and designed by architects Trehearne and Norman Preston & Co, this building is due to be demolished in 2012 despite its inclusion within the Streatham Hill and Streatham High Road Conservation Area, and replaced by a block of flats. The Armistice Ball, seen advertised in this photo, was held at the Locarno in November 1930, when it was one of the most popular purpose-built dance halls in South London. It was renamed The Cat's Whiskers in 1970 and its most recent incarnation until its closure in 2010 was as Caesar's Night Club.

Sparks Garage - Sternhold Avenue - Streatham

John A. Sparks' Garage was a colourful landmark facing the northern flank of Streatham Hill Station at the junction of Blairderry Road and Sternhold Avenue. It was also known as the Windmill Garage because of its distinctive red and blue motif on the Dutch-style gable end on its biscuit-coloured tiled frontage. It survived into the 1980s but was replaced by Wentworth House (Streatham's Job Centre) soon itself to be demolished for the redevelopment of this and the adjacent former Gaumont and Locarno Ballroom sites.

Kennington Lido - Kennington Park

Opened in 1931, Kennington Lido was "paired" with London Fields Lido in Hackney. They had pools of identical size and were more elaborate than previous lidos. They had staff and first aid rooms, individual and group changing rooms and a cafe. The lido was in the south east corner of Kennington Park (which can be seen in the top left corner of this c1939 view). The London Fields Lido has been restored and is very popular today but sadly Kennington's closed in 1988 and games courts now occupy the site.

Former Streatham Assembly Hall and Baths - Streatham High Road

Streatham Baths was designed by Wandsworth Council's Borough Architect, Ernest J. Elford and opened in 1927. It was of a classical 1920s style with brick quoins to the pavilion bays and an imposing Tuscan Doric portico above the stone entrance porch. The fine interiors comprised an entrance hall with decorated plaster ceiling, black and white chequer-board floor and an attractive pool hall (pictured middle left) with elliptical roof, lit by stained glass roundels depicting fish in a pool (see photo below).

The bottom left photo shows the West Streatham Choral Society rehearsing at the Baths demonstrating the original multi-purpose use of the building which included concerts and dances in the winter months when the pool was boarded over.

Sadly the swimming pool closed in 2009 and in spite of being in a conservation area, was demolished in 2011 to make way for the new Streatham Hub development comprising 250 flats, a leisure centre with a swimming pool and an ice rink, and a supermarket.

Streatham Ice Rink - Streatham High Road

Streatham Ice Rink and Streatham Baths stood side by side. The rink was opened in 1931 by the Mayor of Wandsworth, Lieutenant Colonel Arthur Bellamy, and Sir William Lane-Mitchell, MP for Streatham (who are seen in the photo bottom right). Its art deco facade had tall narrow windows embellished with plinths with modern style, floral motifs (seen in bottom left photo), a long canopy and five flagpoles.

The rink could accommodate 1,000 skaters and 3,000 spectators and also had restaurants and a dance floor. It hosted a popular ice hockey club founded in 1932, renamed the Streatham Redskins in 1974.

The unlisted ice rink was closed in December 2011, to be demolished to make way for the new Streatham Hub development, notwithstanding the inclusion of the historic building within the Streatham Hill and Streatham High Road Conservation Area.

Camberwell Odeon - Coldharbour Lane/ Denmark Hill

The Odeon Cinema stood on a large V-shaped site at the corner of Coldharbour Lane and Denmark Hill and was a striking landmark. It was the largest Odeon built in London in the 1930s, with a capacity of some 2,500 patrons. Designed by Andrew Mather (job architect Keith Roberts), it opened in March 1939, a few months before the outbreak of the Second World War.

Unusually for a cinema, it had two entrances on each road (as does the Apollo Victoria Theatre, built as the New Victoria cinema in 1930) with seven shop units within the bull-nose podium on the corner. Each entrance was marked by a slender modernist-style tower clad in pale yellow vitrolite tiles, full-height strips of glazing illuminated at night and proudly emblazoned with illuminated Odeon lettering. The grand foyer had a broad staircase flanked by columns of polished black glass leading up to the fan-shaped auditorium which was decorated with a honeycomb pattern of ventilation grills either side of the proscenium (see right).

The Odeon remained in cinema use for 36 years until July 1975 when it showed its final film "*The Night Porter*" starring Dirk Bogarde and Charlotte Rampling. The building then experienced a slow decline, standing empty for another 18 years except for a six year spell as 'Dirty Dirts', a discount jeans emporium, in the 1980s. It was finally demolished in 1993 and replaced by a block of flats and a chicken restaurant. Both the exterior and interior views were taken soon after it opened in 1939.

Two long-gone features that once stood on the concourse of Waterloo Station

The News Theatre at Waterloo Station was located at the eastern end of the great concourse, adjacent to Platform 1. It was a striking example of art deco cinematic design composed of dramatic curves and bright illuminated signage. Opened in 1934, it showed newsreels all day and evenings. The pay box was at concourse level with patrons ascending the open stairs to the auditorium. By 1960 cartoons had replaced the news films which in turn made way for classic Hollywood movies until its closure in 1970, its last films being Alfred Hitchcock's '*Torn Curtain*' and '*An Inspector Calls*'. It lay unused for 18 years until its demolition in 1988.

The final entry of Lost Lambeth ends this book on a more positive note after this roll call of fine buildings of the inter-war period that have been demolished during the last 40 years. This charming WH Smith's bookstall may be 'lost to Lambeth' but when it was removed in 1978, rather than being destroyed, it was saved for the nation and can be enjoyed to this day at the National Railway Museum in York. These kiosks were once found all over Britain's railway system. The reconstruction of Waterloo Station was completed in 1922 and amongst its many amenities was this splendid timber bookstall - note its wooden roller shutters, the highly varnished stained wood panelling, the curved-glass display window and the dentil course above the fascia.

Index of Inter-War buildings in Lambeth

Abbotswood Road 35
ABC Cinema 41
Acre Lane 15,79,80
Adshead, Professor Stanley 77
Albert Embankment 22,86
Allison, R. 85
Armstrong, Edward 66
Aspen House Open Air School 32
Astoria Cinema 40,42,43
Atkins Road 62
Baines, Frank 46
Balham Maternity Hospital 39
Battersea Grammar School 35
Bawden, Edward 90
Bayes, Gilbert 22,87
Bayliss Road 49
Beacon Bingo 47
Bell Public House 52
Belvedere Road 19
Bennett, T.P. 45,87
Benshurst Court 71
Bentham, P.G. 83
Bernays Grove 88
Bethell, Frank 80
Black Prince Pub 44
Black Prince Road 44,65
Blairderry Road 91
Blomfield, Reginald 56
Bloomfield Cottage Estate 63
Bowling Green Street 34
Boyton House 65
Bridge House 87
Brighton Terrace 88
Bristow, Christopher 30
Brixton Academy 40,42,43
Brixton Astoria Cinema 40,42
Brixton Hill 55,68,69
Brixton Markets 80
Brixton Road 79,81
Brixton School of Building 31
Brixton Village 80
Brixton Waterworks Pumping Station 29
Brockwell Lido 48
Brown, George Lansdown 85
Buckner Road 15,16
Burton, W.H. 47

Burton's 82
Caesar's Night Club 90
Camberwell Odeon 94
Cat's Whiskers 90
Central Hill 25, 57
Century House 83
Chester Way 65
Chichely Street 19
China Walk Estate 58,61
Christchurch House 68
Clapham Common Northside 84
Clapham Common Southside 36
Clapham Common Underground Station .. 54
Clapham High Street 52
Clapham Old Town 72,83
Clapham Park East Estate 62
Clapham Road 28, 78
Cleaver Square 26
Cleaver Street 26
Coldharbour Lane 50,80,94
Cooper, Edwin 36
Cotherstone Road 32
Couch & Coupland 68
County Hall 19-24
David Grieg's Head Offices 84
Dear, Frank T. 28
Denmark Hill 39
Dorchester Court 72
Doulton House 87
Duke of Sussex Public House 49
Dulwich Road 48
Dumbarton Court 68
Dunlop, Dennis 16
Durning Road 63
Edmund Distim Maddick Memorial 28
Edward Maufe 78
Electric Lane 80
Elford, Ernest J. 92
Elsom, Cecil H. 46
Empress Theatre 88
Ferndale Road 31
Forrest, George Topham 55,56
Forum Magna Square 21
Franklin-Wilkins Building 85
Furneaux Avenue 63
Gala Bingo Club 44

Gaumont Palace Cinema 45
Gaumont Super Cinemas 88
George West House 84
Gibberd, Sir Frederick 69
Gibbs Square 63
Gipsy Hill Police Station 25
Gipsy Hill Telephone Exchange 30
Glasshouse Walk 63
Glen, W.R. 41
Gower, Graham 70
Granada Cinema, Granada Bingo 44,46
Grant, M.W. 76
Granville Arcade 80
Granville House 80
Greyhound Lane 51
Greyhound Public House 51
Guthrie Clinic, King's College Hospital ... 39
Hamp, Stanley 39
Harrington, Frank 70,71
Harrison, J.E.K. 35
Henry Fawcett Primary School 34
Herne Hill 72
Hill, Joseph 50
Hioms, F.R. 19
Holden, Charles 18,54
Holy Redeemer, Church of the 76
Horns Tavern Public House 51
Humphreys, George William 56
Israel, Laurence 46
Ivor House 80
James Clerk Maxwell Building 85
Jebb Avenue 29
Jessop Primary School 33,34
Jones, F. Edward 88
Kemp and Tasker 72,75
Kennings Estate 62
Kennington Lane 65
Kennington Lido 91
Kennington Palace Court 64
Kennington Park 53,61,91
Kennington Park Estate 61
Kennington Park Road 49
Kennington Park Rose Garden 53
Kennington Regal Cinema 44
Kennington Road 26,44,61,77
King of Sardinia Public House 51

Entry	Page
King's College	85
Knights Hill	51
L.A. Culliford & Partners	83
Lambeth Bridge	56,86
Lambeth Bridge House	86
Lambeth County Court	26
Lambeth Fire Station	22
Lambeth High Street	24
Lambeth Road	52
Lambeth Town Hall Assembly Room	14-18
Larkhall Estate	67
Latitude Apartment Building	36
LCC Tramways Depot	55
Leigham Avenue	71
Leigham Court Road	71,82
Leigham Hall	70
Locarno Dance Hall	90,91
London Fire Brigade HQ	22
Loughborough Park Estate	66
Lowden Road	33
Lyons, Eric	46
M.R.J. Rundell & Associates	75
Mahoney, Cyril (Charles)	90
Manor Court	71
Maritime House	83
Market Row	80
Mather, Andrew	94
Megabowl	45
Molly Huggins Close	39
Morley College	90
Morton, F.P.	22
Mountearl Gardens	63
New Park Road	68
Newburn Street	64
Newquay House	64
Nicholas, Charles	45
Nicholson, Sir Charles	76
Norwood Park	63
Norwood Regal Cinema	88
Norwood Road	88
Oaklands Estate	62
Old Red Lion Public House	49
Opal Street Estate	59
Orange Coach Station	89
Orchard Primary School	32
Park Hall Road	30
Payne and Wyatt	84
Peach, C. Stanley	85
Picture House (flats)	41
Pite, Arthur Beresford	31
Pite, William	39
Plough Public House	52
Pollard Thomas Architects	48
Polworth Road	57
Poynders Road	62
Pratts & Payne	82
Prince of Wales Public House	50
Pullman Court	69
Quarme, Giles	38
Quilter, Cecil M.	57
Quin and Axten	81
R. Toms & Partners	70,71
Ramsey, Stanley	77
Ravilious, Eric	90
Reading, A.W.	69
Regal Cinema	41,44,88
Reliance Arcade	80
Restormel House	65
Rosendale Road	30
Sancroft Street	64
Scott, Giles Gilbert	19,29
Searle & Searle	84
Segrais, J.J. de	72
Silver, E.R.	14
Simpkins, F.E.	79
Soissons, Louis de	64,65,67
Somers Road	51
South Bank Gym	46
South London Hospital for Women	36
South London Press Building	82
Spain, J.E. Dixon	45
Sparks Garage	91
Sprague, W.G.R.	47
St Anselm's Church	77
St Bede Church for the Deaf	78
St Cloud Road	63
St Gothard Road	63
St John's Hill	35
Stamford Street	85
Sternhold Avenue	91
Stockwell Road	42
Stockwell War Memorial	28
Stone, Edward A.	40,42,52
Streatham Assembly Hall & Baths	92
Streatham Astoria Cinema	40,42
Streatham Common Northside	27
Streatham High Road	40,41,51,70,82,83,92,93
Streatham Hill	45,69,70,71,90
Streatham Hill & Clapham High School	35
Streatham Hill Estate	63
Streatham Hill Theatre	47
Streatham Hub	92,93
Streatham Ice Rink	93
Streatham Odeon	40,42
Streatham Regal/ABC Cinema	41,44
Streatham Vale	76
Streatleigh Court	70
Sunlight Laundry	79
Tamar House	65
Telephone box	29
Telford Court	71
Tesco	36,38
The High	70
The Pavement	72
Thompson, R.J.	39
Thrale Almshouses	57
Tivoli Road	63
Toft, Albert	27
Travers, M.	76
Trehearne and Norman Preston & Co.	90
Trinity Close	72
Tudor Close	69
Tyers Street	63
Vauxhall Gardens Estate	63
Wandsworth Road	46
Wandsworth War Memorial Maternity Home	39
War Memorial, Streatham Common Northside	27
Waterloo News Theatre	95
Waterloo Road	84,85
Waterloo Station	89,95
Waterloo Station Signal Box	89
Wavertree Court	70
Weald, G.	22
Weir Hospital	39
Weir Road	39
Wentworth House	91
West Norwood Cemetery	28
Westminster Br Rd	19,90
WH Smith	85,86,87,95
WH Smith bookstall	95
Wheeler, E.P.	19,22
Whinney, Son and H. Austin Hall	14,16
White Hart Street	62
Wilson, Harry	82
Windmill Garage, Streatham	91
Windrush Square	89
Woolworths, Brixton	79
Wootton Street	60,66
Wornum, George Grey	67
York Road	19,20